MASTER DATER

The "New Normal" Dating Guide
for Finding Love In the Digital Age
Plus 29 Hilarious & Humbling Anecdotes
from a Therapist's Dating Life

By Tasha Jackson, MA, MFT
with Murphy Hooker

tashajackson.com

Cover design by Brad Basham

Book designed by Tom Trapnell

IBSN # 978-0-578-58047-0

Table of Contents

Single, Sassy and Singing Your Own Tune?

A New Love Song Is on The Way, If You Choose It

Pssst, I see what you just did there — *color me impressed* for buying this book on how to be a *Master Dater*. Although many people say they want to change their love life, not everyone is proactive about it so (seriously) I applaud you for doing a little homework on a topic that has mystified a lot of really smart people. Despite what the media, dating apps and most everyone on social media tells you, you really don't have to be young, rich, and famous to have a healthy love life these days. Here's a little secret the *Tinderati* (not to be confused with the Illuminati) won't tell you — real *whole* human beings seem to have an easier time attracting worthy romantic partners than the Instagram glamour pusses of the world. Are you a real human?

Congratulations, you're already way ahead of the curve.

If you're tired of getting ghosted after yet another one-night stand, and are looking for a nice, *hopefully* sexy guy or girl to date — and maybe marry one day — the secret to changing your romance game (for the better) is simply finding a way to forget about all those ghosts in your closet, and be the most genuine version of the "real you" that you can be. Gee, how hard is that?

OK, I admit — it's not always easy!

In fact, for some of us, it might be the hardest thing we will ever do. But don't chicken out now — just because you haven't found your soul mate (or a warm body you can tolerate sharing your bed with for more than one night) doesn't mean you should feel *less* than in the art of love. At some point, all of us get hard up in the love department — that is just part of being human. We've all been dumped and rejected. We've all gotten suckered into thinking someone's shtick was genuine, and not some sexual smokescreen to get laid. We've all found ourselves feeling alone in a coupling. So, if you grabbed this book because you've been around the block a time or twelve — and are so fed up, you're about to log off permanently, pull the sheets over your head and proclaim eternal devotion to your Netflix queue — don't throw in the towel and start your cat collection, just yet. This is just the introduction — *we still have so far to go together.*

As a seasoned professional psychotherapist working in San Francisco, I've had countless clients tell me *"I keep choosing idiots. What is wrong with me?"* Before you back away from getting your tootsies wet completely because you're afraid of belly flopping in the dating pool again, please know that your experience is universal. Sometimes we get lucky in love and sometimes we don't — but we can't leave it all up to that fat little diaper dude's pointy arrow. Cupid is cute, but teaching yourself how to be *Master Dater* will give you more control of your destiny.

I realize this is the point where the author usually expresses her subject matter authority to impress you. Although I totally get the need for you to trust me, I feel authors can sometimes get a little carried away with their credentials so I'll keep this short, sweet, and sincere, and I'll try not to sound too full of myself.

MASTER DATER

Since I was a child, I have been fascinated by the psychology of relationships. I always knew I wanted to be a healer of some kind when I grew up. Now even with a Master's degree and years of psychological counseling under my belt, I'm still fascinated by how we all tick. I truly love seeing people fall in love and transform into the fulfilled humans they always wanted to be.

Besides that, I've also logged thousands of *practical hours* studying relationships in my personal life, "boning up" (as they say) on the issue constantly for decades (bad pun totally intended). Like everyone, my heart has been stomped on and I've stepped on my fair share of hearts, too. I've certainly gotten my (Malcolm Gladwell approved) 10,000 hours in the relationships department, and I'm still at it today — just with a husband, kids, and a few more wrinkles that I like to call signs of wisdom. I'm still just as passionate (as I was the first time I sat in my faux leather therapist's chair) about encouraging my clients not to settle for a lifetime of bad romance (as Lady Gaga once sang) just because you're afraid of being alone.

You deserve so much better. We all do.

Until now, I've rarely discussed my personal life with strangers. Other than a few people who saw me wobbling around the office pregnant years ago, my clients know very little about me. It's not that I purposely withhold information but I've found being a blank slate is best for the therapeutic process. That changes today.

On these pages, I'm exposing myself to you in ways I never have before (not in that way). I'm breaking my therapist code into a million pieces to share a more intimate voice with you. Why the change of heart? I believe personal stories have the power to connect our souls, especially when you hear them directly from the source. Plus, I like getting to know authors along the way — don't you? I enjoy feeling like I'm really hanging out with my authors. I even wish some would include more pictures of themselves, other than the typical (decade old) headshot. Am I the only one??

Also, I feel like you need to know at least a little about my personal life to understand the concepts in this book. Raw data without context can be extremely useful for many fields of study, but in the love department? It can leave you cold. Bullet points are hard to digest without a little color (and context) to wash it down, and rarely stick to the heart — so I'm going out on a limb, and humanizing some of my most relevant lessons on love in order to paint a fuller picture of myself, while hopefully fostering a real human bond between me and you, the reader.

A little caveat before we dive in: the stories in this book are factually accurate, but the clients and friends I mention are composites of people I know, or flat out fictional characters I've used to make a point. Other than the references to myself, any resemblance to a real person is purely coincidental. I even disguised some of my own stories to protect me from some ex-man friend showing up at my office with a freeway billboard lawyer, or a shiv to my tires. Bottom line: this book should be enjoyed as entertainment, and not as professional medical advice. I do not know your situation — nor have I ever met you — although I'm sure you're a lovely person. Please, if you need professional help, there are lots of ways to find it. I encourage you to reach out to one of the many fabulous healing professionals in your town. Don't hesitate.

Remember: they won't seek you out. You need to find them.

Let me end by saying this — I'm not some "know it all" love guru. I'm just a flawed human being who has a blueprint for happiness that seems to work — but I don't have all the answers. By showing you a glimpse into my humanity, I hope you'll see some of yourself in my fumbles, foibles, and triumphs — because I (too) am a work-in-progress who falls on my face occasionally, regardless of my credentials. I simply want to share what I know to help you decode the modern dating landscape and make it a bit simpler for you. I hope you will walk away from this experience feeling better about yourself, especially if you've been spending far too much time looking for your own Shape of Water fish lover. Because unless you're dating a psycho or a fish — whatever is going on in your dating world is not some dysfunctional freak show — the odds are (actually) it's pretty common. We humans are more alike than we like to think.

To get the most out of this experience, I suggest you read *Master Dater* front to back, in its entirety. No flipping! Please don't let it rot on your nightstand next to that box of expired condoms (sorry — that unused box of new condoms). It won't do you any good that way. The last thing I want is for you to copy every move in the book.

The chapters don't work that way!

Think of this book as food for thought.

Let the stories steep into your soul, and once you've soaked them in, I hope you will customize each concept to fit your life. I also hope you will enjoy the ride a little, because (like romance) this book is supposed to be filled with giggles — so go have some fun, and when the time is right, go ahead and cannonball back into the dating pool.

Get in — don't be shy. The water's *perfect*.

With Gratitude,
Tasha

1 Why Even Date, Anymore?

Finding Light at The End of Your Tunnel of Love

I hear this all the time from my single friends, *"Dating is more effort than it's worth. By the end of the day, I'm so tired I can't imagine going on a date; I've given up!"* If this statement sums up your current dating philosophy — I feel you, getting hit in the kisser by a revolving door of douchebags can make you never want to leave your couch again. But as much as Netflix can be a pleasant diversion from your neglected love pump (oh you, I meant your heart!) after a while, you may begin to realize the cast of *Strangers Things* can't go to Bora Bora with you, or whisper sweet nothings in your ear, or give you "all the feels" between the sheets. Don't believe what any overprotective parent or health teacher told you about the lustful perils of sucking face (*and so forth*). *Dating is not some extracurricular activity* you can just skip like wood shop or college, and still be totally fulfilled. That was just B.S. they told us so we wouldn't cut class to go have quickies behind the bleachers. Love is actually, the most (re) productive thing you can do.

Human civilization was built on the gyrating backs of billions of our horniest ancestors — who are you to shun our most fundamental purpose in life? All kidding aside, if you are on an extended voluntary hiatus, I gently urge you not to stay on the sidelines too long. No person can be happy alone on an island unless you're into collecting coconuts or you're a contortionist with (ahem) amazing D.I.Y. B.J. skills), so I want you to avoid thinking like a castaway when there are so many other lovely mercury-free fish in the sea. Finding a new love interest will not solve all your dark "emo" problems — but it's healthy to be in love. Love makes us feel good and gives us someone to share our lives with. *Love takes us out of ourselves*. Besides, you will live longer as a couple than you will alone. Animals don't fare well without love, and neither do humans.

Love connections are vital to our health and happiness. A new lover will not bring you everlasting joy but it's important to keep trying to connect. You will learn something new even from the relationships that don't last. So, put away (Lelo) your vibrating rabbit and *go love somebody* already. We only go around once, don't miss your chance while you're still young. Birds do it. Bees do it. Even educated fleas do it. Now it's your turn to make a little hey-hey. How awesome is that?

2 Dating Out of Your Comfort Zone

Hooked on Bad Boys or Femme Fatales? Try A New Flavor You Never Tasted Before

New relationships can open the door to personal growth in so many unexpected ways. We can heal old emotional wounds by having new experiences with other people. *Dating does that. Love does that. Relationships do that.* And when you least expect it, someone new can waltz into the room and change your life forever. To prepare for serendipity, you need to be open to new things, which can be hard for many people. I know; I'm one of those people! *Dating out of your comfort zone* is a subject that came up for me years ago when an (unwanted) matchmaker friend suggested I meet some "great guy" she knew. I remember feeling defensive at the very idea. I said, *"Thanks, but I can find my own dates, thank you. I'm kind of dating this surfer guy, and that lawyer dude, sort of, and I'm totally flirting with my hot artist neighbor."*

My unwanted matchmaker persisted, *"Do you really see those guys lasting?"*

I gulped my wine. I won't lie; it stung to be put on the spot by several happily married Yentas. It hurt even more when my good friend did not defend me. She just looked away. Ouch. My mind raced, *oh geez, maybe they are right?* My matchmaker showed me a picture and told me all about the great guy's job, and how kind he was.

I took one look. *"He's good looking but a little too vanilla for me. Not my type."*

Seriously, who did I think I was? Giselle? Beyoncé? Rihanna?

"Well, how is 'your type of guy' working out for you?" my nemesis persisted.

I thought — *Not great?* Any remaining ego I had popped like a balloon. I gave my unwanted matchmaker the grumpy cat side-eye the rest of the night, but I agreed to meet the guy. Deep down, I knew what she said was true. I had to cast a wider net and get out of my comfort zone. Flash forward to a week later, and I got to the restaurant before my blind date. I immediately had the silverware removed from the table. I told myself — *You're going to have one drink, and then be out the door.* My fragile ego was going prove my pushy matchmaker friend dead wrong, dammit. Then my blind date walked in ... The first thing he did was ask our server, *"Can I please have some silverware because I would like to have dinner and get to know this beautiful woman in front of me."*

Whoa. I was not expecting that. What else happened?

Was he an overbearing cheese ball?

Did he turn out to be another d-bag "Broseph" in a suit?

Or was he, in fact, my prince charming in disguise?

If so, would I sabotage the opportunity because he didn't fit my type, which I admit is not very realistic, since I'm attracted to malnourished artists like Edward Scissorhands, minus the scissors.

I will leave you guessing for now ... don't give me the grumpy cat face. I'm not doing it because I think my love life is cliffhanger worthy like some Victorian novel. Rather, I feel giving you a little extra time to ponder the outcome of my blind date will allow us to explore (in future chapters) how a few subtle changes to how we perceive our potential mates can make a powerful impact on our dating lives.

If you are stuck in the dating version of the movie *Groundhogs Day*, and you're tired of sleeping with a never-ending stream of single-serving Scissorhands — I hope you will continue to keep an open mind about your dating type, because who we are connected to romantically in life is vital to our health and happiness. The opportunity for emotional and physical connection that dating gives us is healthy, energizing, and should never be taken for granted just because a man or woman doesn't look like Giselle or Tom (or the Italian Scissorhands soccer team, purr purr). So, the next time you feel like retiring from the dating scene to have a fulfilling one-way relationship with one of the Hemsworth brothers, remember this mantra:

We date because we are human.

We date because we feel better being with other people.

We date because making human connections is good for us.

We date new people because it helps us grow as individuals.

Got it? I may test you on this later when I come back to this story …

3 The Last Single Person on Earth?

If I Don't Lower My Standards, Will I Die A Cat Lady?

C an I admit a guilty pleasure? I still like the 90s movie *Swingers* (does that make me weird?) If you haven't seen it, there is a funny scene where the main character (John Favreau) leaves 8 messages in a row on a woman's answering machine that he wants to date. One after another, the messages get more painful as he fumbles with his words. Watching this scene play out makes people cringe because *we've all been there.* Say what you will about the movie, but I feel that moment is a perfect example of how we all universally struggle with how to date. When should we call? What we should wear? How many dates until you get to have sex? These are all totally appropriate questions.

Want to hear one that's not relevant to the conversation?

"If this doesn't work out, will it be my last chance to find love?"

When I hear this question from anyone under 80 — my answer is always, "Not unless you plan on joining a nunnery!" There's this wonderful thing about dating, as long as you have that itch, there are plenty of partners to go around. Dating is not like some *Hunger Games Noah's Ark Dating Service* where, if you strike out, you're jettisoned into space to live with Elon Musk for all eternity

(though I can see the reality series now.)

No, as long as you want to love someone else, and are ready to put yourself out there, you are probably going to get countless shots at finding a willing partner. So, relax. You're not going to die a cat lady obsessing over your frozen eggs (or a doggie daddy forever covered in fur) just because you got ghosted for the umpteenth time. How many dates will it take before you find your true love? Not even the palm reader down the street can predict that, why are you asking me?

The good news is whenever you feel lost, or confused in a dating situation, you don't need to ask a magical soothsayer for help when you already have a fully functional GPS called your moral compass to guide you. Oh yeah — that old dusty thing? *Yes, that old dusty thing.* Since psychotherapists can't legally give out play-by-play instructions on how to date, I strongly encourage you to listen to your ethical compass. Even when a date feels like some clown show you got roped into by a screwball case of mistaken identity — do your best to treat the process with sincerity. Try your best to act with compassion and kindness in those sticky dating moments. Try to be understanding with the people you date, because most of us are trying to do our best out there, but we all come from different starting points, and have acquired different bruises along the way.

As much as it can hurt sometimes, it's not healthy for anyone to treat our modern mating ritual like a 12-round boxing match with a Russian heavyweight where one knockdown means — it's cat lady time. It's just a date; unless your Meghan Markle, trust me, the stakes are not that high! In dating, we can actually get back up off the mat, dust ourselves off, and try again. Even if you just had the worst date of your life, things can turn around in a second. Keep on dating! I wouldn't be a psychotherapist if I didn't truly believe change was possible — it is — I've seen it happen countless times. So, relax, and try to have some fun — because no matter what happens, you will live to love another day.

If you are still feeling a little vulnerable putting yourself out there, I encourage you to work on grounding yourself in a place of compassion, authenticity, and abundance before you dive back into the dating pool. If you can do that, you won't sweat a bad date (or five, *or 50*) because you'll know in your heart there are millions of other options at the love buffet. Getting into this mental space will be a process that can become a personal ritual, but once you're locked into a mindset that is authentically you, you will gain confidence, and start to believe that you are an awesome fucking catch — because, guess what, you are!

There may still be moments when you feel like giving up to join a nunnery or a polyamorous love cult — but if you can just stay patient, and hold true to what your moral compass says feels right, as the decent person I know you are, things have a way of working themselves out.

So, the next time you're on a date, do everyone a favor, and leave your boxing gloves at home, and keep hope alive with the knowledge that there are plenty of other good fish in the sea to share a waterbed with, spawn with, or just get slippery with for a night. Just be sure to treat the other fishies with kindness, and not like some slippery eel that's only looking out for themselves. Who wants to date, marry, or even go to Bed Bath & Beyond with a slippery eel, anyway?

Those sea snakes are the loners of the sea for a reason.

4 Dreaming of a Gosling Prince and Getting a Brony Parade?

Tired of Chasing Unicorns? Try Dating Some Real Humans Instead

Before a first date — do you ever find yourself, daydreaming that some gorgeous specimen like Ryan Gosling or Olivia Wilde is going to ride in on their solid gold unicorns, and put an engagement ring on it? I think we all do this in some way, but I'm not sure it's a good idea to expect a grand slam on your first at-bat. I'm not saying you don't deserve a Perfect 10 — but finding unicorns in the wild rarely happens overnight. Sure, romantic sparks may fly on your first date, or you may have to wait until the 87th humanoid rings your doorbell before you stumble onto your dream boat. But, if you can conjure the patience to convince yourself that *dating is a process*, it will keep you in a healthy mindset to keep searching for love.

I don't want to put any pressure on you but — to make your quest more manageable — I encourage you to (at least consider) being a tad more realistic with your expectations. I've found it can help temper your tender feelings along the way. I really hope your Ryan or Olivia (or whomever it is that lights your f.i.r.e.) will gallop into your life the second you say, *"I think I am ready to date someone new."* But you will probably first have to go on a few dates with some geeks, bros, or even a few "Bronies" (male adult My Little Pony collectors, if you haven't heard) who live in their parent's basement.

I should know; I dated them all. Don't ask!

But even if you share my Brony PTSD — you can't give up on the game just because you realize the men you're dating are more like Ryan Seacrest than Ryan Gosling. That's just life — all I can say is, do your best to laugh off the bizarre dates. Don't fall into the trap of assuming they're all signs that you will die alone, surrounded by meowing fur pillows. If no one got hurt on the date, file the experience away as humorous conversation material, because all of us (even Ryan and Olivia) have to pay our dues to the Dating Gods. So, just think of that bizarre Brony date, where he convinced you to dress up as Pinkie Pie Pony at 3am as a substantial offering to the Gods, and move on.

We all have big dreams, so the last thing I want to do is burst anyone's bubble — but if you're currently building a Gosling Shrine in your bedroom instead of accepting an offer to have dinner with that nice coworker who seems fairly cool but a little boring — I gently urge you stop expecting the real Ryan or Olivia to walk through the door. Try dating real humans instead. I'm not saying it will never happen, but why not see what you can do with the cards you've been dealt?

Maybe you will discover that dating a solid 6 who has a high ceiling for improvement is actually pretty awesome? Why not explore that option instead of watching *The Notebook* for the 20th time? Because, as much as we all enjoy dating physically beautiful people, true love rarely comes in the package you expect. Love stories tend to be surprising with lots of twists and turns, but it will never happen to you unless you allow yourself to be *open to being surprised.*

Now, if you are still determined to attract a Perfect 10, know that you are going to face stiff competition, and it will probably entail you dating a lot of *Justin Timberfakes* and *Johnny Schlepps* before you find the real deal — but it can happen, maybe.

What if you never find your sweet golden unicorn?

Don't despair. Right now, there is someone out there who checks a lot of the boxes on your vision board — who thinks you, and all your flaws, *are that Perfect 10*. Ryan and Olivia are great, but wouldn't you like to meet a real person who adores you like you do them? As long as he or she isn't a cartoon horse addict — I encourage you not to pass that opportunity up because, if you ask me, being treated like a Perfect 10 by a real *human being who you really love* is much better than dating a high-maintenance unicorn. Sure, they're gorgeous — but they tend to take up all of the "air space" in a relationship, not to mention, monopolize all the mirrors and compliments.

And have you seen their table manners?

It's like they were raised in a magical barn. Oh wait. They were.

5 Should I Blowtorch My Vision Board?

Experiment with Dating and Set Your Own Rules for the Game of Love

Recently I was having dinner with friends over a flight of wine, yes, *again* — don't judge — where the conversation centered around a friend who told us she was getting more dates after one of her three cats died. The question of the evening became: *If you had to date someone with three cats, or six stuffed animals on their bed — which would you choose?* Surprisingly, my male dinner guests preferred the person with the six stuffed animals. They felt three actual cats was a sign something was wrong with the cat owner. Maybe they assumed if they dated a cat lady, they'd be forced to have feline tea parties every night before bed? I never understood why they drew that particular line in the sand (2 cats? Normal. 3 cats? Crazy pants!) but our poll was unanimous — so there you have it, ladies. Get a third cat and you're entering the spinster zone. Who knew for some men, there was actually such a thing as too much pussy?

I only bring up the cat conversation because it seems a lot of people today are quite comfortable having their own highly-curated list of "must-haves" for a potential partner, which I feel, ties into our society's obsession with Perfect 10s, and unrealistic vision boards. Now, I realize there are many smart people who strongly believe having an Oprah-approved vision board helps them to spiritually welcome (i.e. manifest) positive energy and (yes) dream partners into their life, which is a valid argument. But to me, it also (kinda) feels like a question you get while reading *Cosmopolitan* magazine: "What's your checklist for your ideal mate?" Quick: let me get my craft's kit!

Let's see: tall, dark, handsome, oozes money, and speaks Italian while making love to me all day and night? Check to all of that! But as fun as it is to build a grand vision board, what is the actual likelihood that my Perfect 10 sex fantasy will ever materialize on planet earth, or more specifically, in my bed? And if the odds of that happening are similar to winning the lottery, should I spend all this time building a shrine to my wildly unrealistic expectations?

Won't that add to my disappointment when my fantasy doesn't come true?

First, let me just say, there is nothing wrong with having a non-obsessive "light" version of a romantic vision board, or wanting your life partner to be sane, stable, want kids, or have a lucrative job that doesn't involve selling major hallucinogens. But I'm noticing, particularly nowadays, a lot of people are ignoring their practical wish list for a future partner, in order to practice *full on magical thinking*.

I meet so many people in my practice today who think they can magically deal with their partner's defective personality trait (which already drives them nuts) or overlook a life dream, while assuming they can mold their partner's beliefs to theirs. This is the classic *"I can change my flawed partner"* line of thinking. I've seen it in action and it almost always goes "Poof" once it's tested in the real world. I've had clients who were married for 15+ years come to me totally miserable, and say, *"I can't believe it. I thought they were going to change."* Sadly, you can probably guess, unions based on magical thinking rarely (if ever) work out. So I honestly, do not want you to settle. (When you do not fully respect a person, it will eventually come out.)

Whatever your romantic vision board looks like today — I encourage you to resist the urge to practice magical thinking on your unsuspecting dates. Stick to the facts, ma'am. I'm not saying blow it up entirely, but try whittling your vision board down to an essential list of "must-haves," and then make them part of your internal compass, and be sure to test them constantly because your desires will probably change over time. For example, as you grow older, falling in love with a single parent may not be such a deal breaker. Maybe as you enter your 30s, it actually fills a need? Being a stepparent is rarely anyone's first choice, but when you're in a good situation, it can work quite beautifully.

If your grand vision board keeps getting in the way of finding a steady partner, I invite you to also think about *what it means to even date?* Try to evolve your mindset a little, because the people I've met who claim they love to date around (yes, I said that right) tend to have a few things in common. Want to know what they are?

First, the "happy-to- daters" are usually extroverts who thrive on making new connections. This doesn't mean you can't enjoy dating if you're an introvert; but a part of you (kind of) has to enjoy meeting new people. Second, they didn't consider every date to be potential marriage material; they simply viewed them as a chance to meet new people. Finally, healthy daters did not view bad dates as signs of doom, or that they were un-loveable — they simply deemed them "not good fits" and moved on. Whether their date became a romantic relationship, a career networking opportunity, or a total bust — they still kept putting themselves out there.

Now, being a natural introvert myself, I realize not everyone can snap their fingers and adopt this mindset, but I encourage you to find a mental space that works for you. And if you're still not having luck, why not temporarily set aside your hyper-focused vision board goals of meeting (say) a great lay, or finding a baby daddy — and try experimenting with your intention for each date? What do I mean?

One date can be an opportunity to branch out, and hear a different life story. Another can be a chance to explore your town through another person's shoes, or an opportunity to try a new cuisine. Experimenting with dating and altering your vision board (if not burning it entirely!) opens your mind to people and experiences you may never have on your own. It also relieves some of that self-induced pressure.

If I can ask one thing from you, it would be this: even when experimenting with dating, try to be as honest as possible with the people you date. Try not to waste their time and be sensitive to their feelings. I really mean that — practice good love karma. And if your experimentation doesn't feel right — that's OK too. *Now you know where you draw the line.* See how this experimentation thing works?

Now you *try*.

6 The Seinfeld Curse: The Superficial Quest for Real & Fantastic

Consider Dating Out of Your Perfect Zone: You Might Be Amazed What You Find

We expect so much out of our partners today, is it too much? Happy unions are no longer about bearing children, or tending to a respectable herd of sheep — with fertility clinics and *Whole Foods* home delivery available — raising herds of kids or sheep isn't exactly what most Americans seek these out of marriages, these days. Today, we want our partners to be our best friends, have the same values, hobbies, ambitions, to be beautiful, great in bed, a great provider, an awesome parent, and to bring you your coffee exactly the way you want it every morning at 6am, right?

I've actually had a friend tell me they weren't going to date someone because they saw an Instagram post of the person drinking a latte from Starbucks. Seriously? Their rationale was *"it indicates their lack of knowledge of how big corporations are destroying the world, that paper cup represents their lack of environmentalism."* Hey, I'm not judging anyone here; I'm merely describing the moment because I bet most of us modern humans make plenty of rash (dare I say misguided?) judgments about strangers, and (definitely) potential sex partners. I mean c'mon, it's what we do these days. We all seem to have our own version of a syndrome I call the *Seinfeld Curse.*

What the hell is that? This is just my theory, but it seems our culture took its cues from that popular TV show 20 years ago, and now we're all are a bunch of Jerry's, running around demanding "only the best" of everything (be it partners, jobs, homes, vacations, food, friends, or stuff in general). This desire to surround ourselves with only the best is perfectly fine if you have the means to procure what you want, but if you don't (like most of us?) I feel our extremely high standards are getting in the way of finding real humans to date. Now that you've read the last few chapters, if you're now saying to yourself — OK, I get it. I need to lower my expectations a bit, but which "must have" can I take off my vision board without selling out my dreams?

It's a great question. I wish I had the perfect answer.

One thing I can tell you is hyperactive idealism can lead to disappointment and isolation since no real person can live up to someone's impossibly high standards. I also know that too much settling can leave you miserable, and always wondering "What if?" No one ever wants to settle for less, if the whole package is realistically out there.

But, is it? Will you throw this book at the nearest wall if I say — yes and no?

What I mean is, you may never find the "real and fantastic" you've been pining for, but if you can look past the outer persona of (say) a person you thought you'd never date — you may discover they're not so un-dateable, after all. They may not be perfect unicorns, but maybe, being with a sailor is more anchoring than you thought, or dating that "boring" banker is actually really creative and fun? Or perhaps that atheist you're seeing is actually the most moral person you ever met?

If you remember my blind date cliffhanger (more on that later) — if it wasn't for my matchmaker pushing me out of my comfort zone, I would've never given that guy a chance. At the time, I remember wondering — *are our (very American) cultural standards to only date rich genius hotties getting in the way of finding real partners?*

In retrospect, how could it not??

Because the hard truth is, while we are all running around searching for perfect people to date, many happy marriages are created when people simply allow themselves to fall for "the girl next door," or "the nice guy." What can we learn from their happiness? *You can still love someone who doesn't fit your perfect image.*

Sure, we all want to find ideal partners that please our parents and our friends. There is nothing wrong with wanting to marry a person that your tribe will think is a catch — we all want to "date up" the food chain. But if you keep running into brick walls, try asking yourself — *What led me to think I could only be attracted to that certain type in the first place?* Was it friends, books, TV, freaking *Seinfeld*, or the Internet that helped form your opinion? If you realize, "Actually yeah, it kinda was," you're not alone.

I will never tell you what to do, butttt — maybe it's time to forget about your loftiest standards for a while, and just let your heart lead the way? See what magic the Love Gods have in store for you! You may not find your picture-perfect dreamboat, but if you are open to it — *love will surprise you, every time.*

7 Desperately Seeking Someone That's Just Not There?

Projecting Your Ideals on a Blank Screen Never Ends Well

Years ago, I was traveling overseas with a good friend. We would entertain ourselves with an improvisational game. Often, it would happen while we were waiting for a train, or struggling with a travel mishap, and needed to lighten the mood. So, we'd sit down and size up strangers. We were very discrete so no feeling got hurt, but we would make up funny stories about people, often including some outlandish dialogue. The goal was to make each other laugh at some ridiculous tall tale about how a stranger (really) was a famed nail fungus hunter, or the cult leader of an underground Sudoku training group. It was just our way of getting through a bad 3rd world transportation day, but it was also a gamed-up version on what psychotherapist's call "projecting"

Projecting happens *all the time* in real life, often without people knowing they're doing it. We project by assuming things about other people based on their looks. We project by placing meaning on other people's actions. We project what somebody else's body language says about their current mood. Our projections are usually pulled from our assumptions, bias, our own life history, or what we want, or fear to be true.

In dating — projections are always part of the fantasy, and often part of a relationship's downfall. Perhaps it's our primal urge to procreate, but there is something in our brains that allows us to fall in love with just "the idea" of someone else, rather than the actual person. People can fall in love with only a profile picture these days! It's almost like our brains are tricking us into having sex, just so we can keep the human race populated. How sick is that? Whether that is 100% true, or not — guess what usually happens with projections? They almost never match up with reality.

I have fallen prey to projections many times in my love life. You probably have too. The last time it happened to me was a few years ago when I was in the middle of taking some time off from dating. Love wasn't even on my radar until one night when I went to a holiday party. I was recovering from knee surgery, still on crutches, and totally immobile so I couldn't escape socializing. As an introvert, I felt like social prey with a big target on my back. I knew I would be helpless when someone came over to talk to me. It's not like I could casually sneak off on crutches, so I just sucked it up and smiled.

Then it happened.

This stylish, sexy-looking guy approached me and started chatting me up. I thought he was cute and well spoken. I wasn't blown over, but even if I wanted to escape, I had no choice! I was forced to converse with him all night. We bonded over being college athletes, laughed over silly culture mannerisms, and explored the various places we'd both traveled. When the party ended, he walked me (and my crutches) home through the North Beach neighborhood of San Francisco. We exchanged phone numbers and had an extended PG-13 kiss (which is all I will divulge of that).

I thought it was a pretty fun night, but for various reasons, I didn't think much about it. After all, the guy said point blank, *"I'm just out of a relationship and am emotionally unavailable."* So, I wrote him off.

But the next day, my curious roommates wanted to know who that cute guy was that walked me home? So, we got online, and hunted him down like we were in the FBI. We discovered the guy seemed to check a lot of the boxes on my metaphoric vision board. Simply because my friends were so enthusiastic about him, I quickly went from a *"That was fun"* to *"Wow, maybe I should pursue him?"* Just by looking at his social media profile, and seeing his creative career choice, I immediately projected that he must be a really cool guy, which led me to date him for a little while. He was really handsome, well-educated, came from a (seemingly) good family, was successful, kind, worldly, he surfed, and he was artistic. I'm sure Cosmo would've said I had it all!

But I didn't have it all.

Even though he looked good "on paper," when we were together, it was never that easy. We often misunderstood each other. At times, he would be engaging, other times, I felt totally alone in the relationship. After a few months, I realized I was reaching for something that was *just not there.* I saw myself projecting *who I wanted him to be onto him,* but the truth was — we didn't have much chemistry together. If our relationship had a spirit animal it was a mole, or aardvark. Blah gray, of questionable demeanor, we saw moments of the sun, but usually hid in the dark. You wanted to like us but you just didn't know how ...

In the end, our short-lived romance was cuter in concept than reality. Although he warned me (repeatedly) he did not want a relationship, I chose to practice magical thinking instead of facing reality. I projected like a freaking IMAX screen.

I thought — *No I will change him. Just you watch!* Ugh.

Before this experience opened my eyes for good, I always thought if I worked hard enough, I could achieve anything in life, which worked out great in other areas like my profession, or my college sports career — so why not with dating, too?

As unfair as it sounds, love is not a meritocracy.

The hardest workers do not win the best partners.

Looking back, I could call that guy an emotionally dead douche-bag but he did nothing wrong. He was just being himself and I was living in another universe.

I learned a tough lesson that day.

I needed to look at myself — so I took a long hard look at my own tendency to project. I realized that dating is rife with projections no matter who you are. Projections can be small like assuming someone you like belongs to the same political party. Or huge like — by your actions I can see you don't love me anymore!

Projecting may help convince yourself that you "really know" someone, or it may help you get laid — but I've found it's not all that helpful when finding your true love. We all know how it feels when someone else misinterprets our feelings, or thinks we are someone we're not. *It stings.* It also leads to friction and misconnections (and not the good craigslist "Missed Connections" kind) — so do your best not to play the projection game! Try to take people for who they are, and not who you want them to be.

And when you're getting to know someone for the first time? Be mindful of the self-image they project. Don't just accept it at face value. If you are romantically interested, slow your roll a little, and compare their patter to what your (actual) experience is being with the person. If your hot new date seems to be a walking contradiction from Day 1, I suggest you believe what you see, and not what you hear because projecting onto a blank screen almost never ends well, unless you're working at a movie theater. They still have those, right? They must, right?

Oh wait, I'm projecting again.

8 Get Whole, Get Confident & Get Your Tight Pants On

Return to the Singles Pool with Style, Savvy, and Swag

Most of us have probably heard this old therapy axiom: *knowing what you want out of life is essential to happiness.* But have you also heard it can be *pretty hot* when you flash that knowing confidence around the genetic dating pool? Even more than having a smoking summer bod — being a whole, fully-realized version of yourself attracts people to you like a pheromonal magnet. I equate *achieving wholeness* to feeling like Will Ferrell with his tight pants on (if you haven't seen him on *The Tonight Show* in his tight pants, Google it for a laugh). Whether you're into his comedy or not, you gotta admit, the man owns every scene. You can sense his confidence through the screen; you can almost smell it. Whether his act kills or bombs, he doesn't need validation from anyone to remain centered in his own skin. I wouldn't call Will Ferrell a hottie (per se), but throw in those tight pants plus his "whole swagger" and (I can't believe I'm saying this) but he's *almost* Gosling sexy, if you're into middle-aged comedians with dad bods.

That's what *feeling whole* can do for you — you can look like Will Ferrell, and still vibe like Ryan Gosling. You may be asking

— OK, well how can I replicate the whole Ferrell mojo so I'm strutting around in my own tight pants? You don't have to shop at Whole Foods, have a fat bank account, or that banging beach body to achieve wholeness. *Being whole* simply means feeling confident and secure in your own life path and place in the world. It means loving yourself so much that you're less likely to be judgmental of others, which will attract others to you. *Being whole* doesn't mean you have all the answers, it means you're asking *all the right questions.* That is *hot.*

A graduate professor of mine once told me humans often get in relationships with people who are at their same psychological level. I have no data to back this up, other than seeing it *all the time* in my practice and personal life. So, yeah, I'm a believer: *the more whole we are, the more likely we are to attract whole partners,* which is far better (IMO) than attracting another person who's fun to play with for a while but is uncaring, unreliable, and breaks as often as a toy in a McDonald's Happy Meal.

I fully admit, I'm not the most together person you'll ever meet — trust me, I'm not — but I do know a lot of well-rounded (whole) people; I even counsel a few, if you can believe that. I've found once whole people finally get it together, they tend to stop taking on, let's call them, "fragmented" lovers, as projects. They also stop being doormats because they respect themselves too much to go through that pain again.

I know — you're still waiting for my *magic bullet cure* to achieving wholeness. I wish I had a universal blueprint but we all have different holes in our games. All I can say is I encourage you to identify then deal with your biggest hang-ups (whatever they may be). If you need to see a therapist to work through your issues — do it. Because once you get whole, you may find that you suddenly stop attracting emotionally abusive jerks, because you just don't have time for their B.S. anymore.

You see, there is no "playing games" when dating whole people. Whole people don't obsess over bad dates because they have plenty of other passions, and a community of friends to keep them feeling whole. They don't expect their lovers to fill them up, because they're already full from living amazing lives. Whole people *fill their own holes* (that didn't come out exactly right, but you get my point!)

If you want to attract partners who have their lives together — spend some time rounding out your own act. Try to spot any low-hanging skeletons lurking in your closet. Work through those mommy or daddy issues you've been stuffing down like a Thanksgiving turkey since the Clinton Administration. Untangle those scars from the mean girls in high school that didn't let you play their reindeer games, or the heartless lover that left you at the altar. Know that, your personal baggage may seem safely hidden away to you, when it's glaringly obvious to the rest of the world.

If you're just now realizing you've got a piece (or two) missing from your "mosaic of self" — you can still get yourself whole again (and put your tight pants on) by some careful, yet gentle, self-examination. Do your best to embrace how traumatic life events affected you. Be honest with yourself. I'm not saying you have to become fully enlightened to attract a worthy mate (though that would be nice) — just see if you can discover who you've become and *who you are on your way to becoming* — and try to set some life goals while you are at it. Get passionate about something. If you can do all that, I think you will discover you're slowly slipping into your tight pants by building up your own confidence and not waiting for the outside world to do it.

One of the biggest ironies about love is once we feel we don't need a lover to validate us, is exactly when someone special will come our way. People tend to find true love when they're content and not looking, which (in my professional opinion) probably has something to do with feeling "whole." It just seems to give people a greater capacity to have emotionally connected relationships with other whole people.

What's that famous Oscar Wilde quote? *"To love oneself is the beginning of a lifelong romance?"* It's so true because if you can't get yourself whole — what chance does some other person have of *completing you?*

9 The Good, The Bad, And The — I Never Would Have Thought About That — of Online Dating

I thank my lucky stars that I met my husband before I was forced to dip my timid toes into the mystifying waters of on-line dating, because (full disclosure) I would've been a self-de-structive mess in a virtual candy store. My combination of shyness mixed with my chronic daydreaming and uber-competitiveness — I can only imagine online dating would have (likely) resulted in me waking up in a pool of my own vomit kind of ugly. Not that I'd be binge drinking my way through dating every Bumble boy that buzzed my way.

I'm talking about more metaphorical kind of vomit.

This is how online dating would have been for me: after one of my "victims" surfaced, I would've started projecting like crazy that they were perfect specimens while beginning to lightly stalk them from every device I could get my sweaty hands on. By the time we went out, I'd be such a wreck that he would spend the evening conversing with my forehead (I'd have my head down all night, due to shyness) except when I was returning from throwing up in the bathroom from nerves.

Gee, put it that way and it's amazing I met anyone in real life. I sometimes wonder — could a dating app do a better job at playing matchmaker than real humans? It's a timely question because, for better or worse, dating site algorithms seem to have replaced traditional matchmakers (like friends, family, and coworkers) as well as our traditional matchmaking institutions (like bars, parties, beaches, cafes, parks, street fairs, bookstores, produce aisles, sex toy stores). Ahem — you get the idea. Yes, it seems everyone who is anyone under the age of 35 is dating online today.

Is our civilization's future in the hands of an algorithm? Are we all doomed?

First, let me just say "*Bravo*" to all of you former "analog daters" who adapted your love lives to the changing times. Although I'm an online dating virgin, I can empathize with the mixture of fear, excitement, horniness, and heartache that dating apps must bring about in even the most confident daters. A few clicks and suddenly you're connected to a sexy stranger. It's a love connection! But … what if he's a psycho? A d-bag? A fuck boy?

Or even worse: what if he's my prince charming who's going to break my heart?

Even if you've never been on a dating app, I feel like online dating has changed our collective brains, as well as our expectations, our patience, and our libidos in so many curious ways. Let's start with the good effects of online dating; there are many.

The biggest upside is they allow people to cast a much wider net than before the Internet. Before apps like Tinder, Match, OK Cupid, Bumble and Grinder, you'd be lucky to hit on all the eligible hotties in a 5-mile radius of your home (or work) in a lifetime. Now you can hit on (practically) every single person in town in a few weeks, if you're feeling particularly ambitious or sex-deprived. As for whether your online dating net catches anything of worth?

That's entirely up to you, but I'm sure we all know someone who has found their soulmates online. If not, check out the married announcements in *The New York Times*. They are everywhere.

Yes, for many people today these apps are amazing because they instantly connect people with other like-minded singles, which can make dating feel spontaneous and fun. I've witnessed several clients use dating apps to be social, increase their personal network, or help them break out of personal funks. When one of my clients Talia, told me, *"I've made it my life goal to go out on three different online dates a week. It gets me out of hotel rooms when I travel for work and who knows what will happen?"* Well, guess what happened? Talia met someone amazing — so online dating rules, right?

I hate to burst anyone's bubble, but as great as it feels to have a virtual sex buffet in your pocket 24/7, never forget that your personal life is a business to dating apps, which means they probably had the next round of Venture Capital funding in mind (and not your future children) when they matched you up with that cute graduate student who may not be chronically employed, but looks like he could show you a good time for one night. Similar to the privatization of healthcare, when corporate monetization seeps into our love lives via dating apps, it should shock no one that (yeah) this kinda affects how we date. Not that love or sex is any different when procured through a dating site, but I feel like many of the apps are set up like slot machines, which can leave people who don't hit the jackpot, feeling a little emotionally broken.

If I just described you, I'm sorry you had a bad experience, but you're not alone. Dating sites just don't seem very interested in true love, they'd much rather prefer you keep coming back to their love buffet again and again. If you're going to rely on dating apps, it seems you (almost) have to play a numbers game and "volume date" to find a love connection, like Talia. Because although dating apps say they want to help you find your soulmate, they (kinda) really just want to help you get laid repeatedly, which would make them the world's top dating app, right? They're not being heartless or cruel I don't think — it's *just business*, babe. Modern love is a casino and we're all living in it.

Knowing that, if I were still single, I wouldn't give up on online dating just yet, because (duh) that's where all the action is. If you've had a horrible experience, the odds are good that it won't be a dating disaster every time. So, you have my blessing, digital daters. In love, you just never know. I've seen so many interesting plot twists transpire for many would-be-romantics; it's almost like logic doesn't play a role in love. When you least expect it, all I can say is — *expect it*. Online dating is not perfect, but it opens so many more doors that would not otherwise be available in the 21st century.

What do you think, you're actually going to pick up a soulmate at the grocery store, a bookstore, or the freaking Farmer's Market? Uh, that actually could happen!

For all you hormonal singles looking for someone to love, I say, enjoy your online dating but don't give up on the real-world hook-up-hot-spots, either, like that Farmer's Market by your house. I'm not trying to convince you to flirt more in the real world, but it is where a little artful fruit and veggie squeezing can become a mating ritual. And who doesn't enjoy hearing classically bad pickup lines like "mine's bigger," "rounder," or "juicier," while *not* receiving an unsolicited dick pic along with it? Get the hint, guys?

10 So Much Swiping, So Much Anxiety

Too Many Choices Can Lead to Dating FOMO or (Even Worse) Eternal Meh Syndrome

C all them relics, call them dating dinosaurs, call them anyone born before 19 freaking 80 — but some people I know believe dating apps take away from the excitement of meeting someone naturally in real life (IRL) without the swipe of a finger, through (say) a mutual friend or acquaintance. Their logic goes, if you meet someone new at a wedding, the bride or groom must've thought enough of them to invite them, so they're probably not *The Golden State Killer*, and (thus) are verified as potential long-term sex partners. I'm not going to choose a side in the "online versus real life" dating debate (since they both do the job) — but I will say, what I find troubling about online dating is it seems to have affected the "emotional vulnerability meters" of some people who actively use them. I have no empirical data on this, but after speaking with clients who use dating apps, I feel like heavy users may lose some of their humanity, because they've gotten so used to treating people like commodities, and not like individuals with real feelings.

Since comparing our lives with others has become an epidemic on social media, why should we be shocked when the same mind-set seeps into our online dating? We all know it's so easy to judge others harshly from behind a screen. It seems like people today "ghost" people faster on dating sites than they would if they had to break up with them in real life. You'll know you've been affected by this modern phenomenon when you find yourself scrolling through a dating app saying things like — *"Meh, he's hot and cool — and his sexts are sexy enough, but they lack originality and wit — so forget him! Or, sure he's a genius with a great job and a great smile, but did you see that Star Trek action figure hiding in the background of his profile picture? Next!"*

That's life at the love buffet where everyone is disposable.

I don't want to get all judgey (I know, too late, right?) but I'm not sure it's all that healthy to compare someone you're dating with profile pictures of people you haven't even met or messaged yet. Talk about the grass always being greener — no one (alive) can compare to a photoshopped avatar! Anyone can seem perfect when posed on the deck of a yacht, especially when compared to that real date you just had where you had to face reality in the form of another real person who may talk too much, have odd fashion sense, or really enjoys toothpicks after a meal. Who wants a real human when you can live in a perpetual state of promised perfection just around the bend?

Here's an example of what I mean: when one of my clients (Ian) started dating Karen on a dating app, he said, *"I'm interested, but not sure what's in store for us."* When they started dating, Ian didn't delete his dating app since they'd agreed not to be exclusive. So, Ian kept checking it out of habit *"when bored."* Next time we met, Ian confessed, *"All these Tinder profiles make everyone seem so cool; I want to date them all."* He called it dating FOMO (Fear of

Missing Out), which I felt was pretty accurate, because although he and Karen were in the fresh freakin' bloom of romance, Ian admitted he was constantly looking over her shoulder to check his phone, asking himself, *"What if? What if? What if?"* His projections went into overdrive.

Last I heard, Ian and Karen had split up. He was still using dating apps, but confessed he might be addicted or desensitized, or something — because now he's unable to be satisfied with any single woman. Geez, how can he? When he's constantly being distracted by an endless stream of sexy avatars 24/7 like he was a sheik with his pick of the harem? That sounds crazy, but it's how a lot of guys feel about online dating.

I've also had female clients (like Lori) tell me that singles on dating apps were there for fun, but were not really giving each other a chance to stick around. *"If you don't have an epic date every time — you're out. Or if you start to get to know each other, then have a little miscommunication — see you later! I've done it too. Why should anyone settle for less than perfect when they can have a new date in an hour?"*

Now if you are at the stage in life where volume dating appeals to you, go ahead and treat other people's bodies like a John Mayer wonderland on dating apps. I don't blame you; I would've done it too (probably). All I'm saying is it's so-so easy to get stuck in a vicious cycle called the *paradox of choice* — where you have so many dating options, none of them seems acceptable. Barry Schwartz wrote a great book about it (by the same name) and had a TED talk about it. Boiled down, his message was we get anxious when we have too many choices. So, if we make the wrong choice, we blame ourselves. *How the hell did I screw that up when I had a million options??* Most humans don't want to think of other people as products, but the idea of having too many choices may be playing on our collective psyches.

All of us want to choose the right mates, but most people today seem to base their decision purely on *what feels good right now*, and not what their brains are telling them *may feel good down the road*, which can lead to heaps of regrets when the smoke clears on your hot date. On top of all that — when apps constantly tease us with (yet) another perfect match, or another text from some randy avatar — it prevents people (like Ian and Karen) from giving each other a chance. Why stick around for any bumps in the road when you can move on to a new catch (who doesn't know your faults, and you don't know theirs?) Many singles today (mostly men) are perfectly happy with these single-serving relationships — so is this our future? Are dating apps turning us all into serial daters who are emotionally unavailable to the real thing?

Not everyone feels there are too many choices in the dating world. Even with a dozen dating apps on your smartphone, if you are remotely selective, it can still feel like you're choosing from a bunch of duds at the bottom of the genetic barrel.

If you're stuck in an online dating rut where no one looks appealing long-term anymore, I encourage you to be mindful of how online dating has affected your empathy for others, especially when you feel like ghosting that dude because he didn't know what a salad fork was last night. This is my gentle reminder to do your best not to treat people like avatars. Rely on your moral compass when casting your net. Try to be open and empathetic to the new people you encounter (online or IRL) even if they don't fit the bill for a typical lover. Many beautiful love connections can happen when we're waiting for another ship to come in — but only if we're ready, and not walking around with our heads stuck in a device 24/7. Whatever you choose, be open for anything, and if you think that new person has potential, give it time for the relationship to unfold. Be patient. Be kind. Be the person you wish all the jerks on Tinder were, so, at minimum, you're not left feeling anxious about how you treated other people — because if you're like most online daters, you already have enough FOMO anxiety to deal with. Am I right??

11 But You Want It All *Dammit*

Corsets, Cryptocurrency, and Courtship Can Co-exist — Rejoice!

A good friend of mine recently had his girlfriend (who worked in the travel industry) take him on a lavish get-away to a 5-star resort. When he returned, relaxed and tanned, he wanted to tell me all about it over dinner. On our way to eat, I noticed before we walked into the restaurant, he stopped by a mailbox to drop her a simple, handwritten thank you note. I was so impressed. I thought good manners had gone the way of the flip phone, Google glasses, or the Roseanne reboot. I was happy to see that a few well-bred souls (like my friend) were still carrying that tradition forward — I wish more people did. This may sound a little old-fashioned to anyone under 30, but if you want to land the lover of your dreams — perhaps consider unveiling some charm and manners on them, and see where that gets you. You might be surprised how far.

I know, comporting yourself like you were *not raised in a barn*, doesn't sound like much, but in a time when many of us feel like it's totally appropriate to floss our teeth or trim our fingernails in public (eww), your good manners will stand out among all the others who are just looking for a bootie call, and don't give a fly-ing fig about decorum. Some may laugh at this notion (go ahead)

— but you really can have a fun, modern courtship while still holding on to some traditional manners and elegance.

Dating apps and good manners are not mutually exclusive.

You really don't have to treat people like dirt online just because you can get away with it. Small courtesies are still valued and appreciated, especially now, when exhibiting good manners is (sadly) often misconstrued as a sign of weakness by the savage hordes who have seemingly taken over our country. I won't name names (that would be rude) … but you know who you are.

If you were never taught manners growing up, you may feel at a slight disadvantage here, but it's not as hard as it seems. Being polite doesn't take much time to pull off, but it can have a huge impact on your love life. Kind gestures like sending flowers, writing thank you cards, and opening car doors can move mountains on a date. Flash some manners over dinner, and I guarantee your partner will feel more appreciated, pampered, as well as a little safer in your presence.

You see, when you are dating a new person, you're both constantly building and breaking trust with each other — so being fully present (and attentive) with another person fosters trust, and (yesss) is sexy beyond words. Showing genuine interest never goes out of style. Listening never goes out of style. Acting like a gentleman or gentle lady never grows old. That's why so many grown women still tune in to Royal Weddings, guys.

We don't miss the misogyny but we do miss being treated special!

Now if you're idea of class is wearing a fresh lobster bib and tuxedo t-shirt to the pizza buffet (no judgments) and you're looking for some hot tips on how to pamper a date — you may want to familiarize yourself with a book or two by Emily Post (a renowned expert on etiquette). But since I've lured you into this conversation, let me offer you a few humble ideas to get you started.

First, I can't believe I have to say this, but put some thought into a date.

Instead of calling a Lyft Share like a cheap bastard, why not splurge the extra $20 bucks and order a luxury black Uber to pick her up instead? And when the special moment comes to consummate your feelings for her, *why not ask permission*, before you plant one on her? This may sound like basic stuff — but it's not for many, many, many (OK men). I'll just say it. From what I've gleaned from my single clients, I feel putting extra thought into a date is becoming a lost art, so when you unveil your inner Southern gentleman (for example) on an unsuspecting date — it will likely take her by surprise, and may even catapult your relationship to a new level, by showing her that you don't eat with your toes, and may have some character hiding under that gruff exterior.

Here's another tip: after you have your next round of good sex, try calling the person the next day and thank them for the good time. Don't Snapchat it, or text a crying freaking eggplant emoji. Try using your lips and just say it — because technology can either close or opens doors for us. Good manners will keep that door open a little longer. I can't force anyone to run a comb through their beard, shave their legs, open some doors, or wear clean underwear — so I will simply encourage you to mix in some old-fashioned courtship to your online dating ritual. You really can wear sexy corsets on dates with techies who pay with cryptocurrency, and still have memorable courtships.

Those two worlds can co-exist, if you want them to.

Warm and fuzzy, feel good hormones (that bond humans together) are released with eye-to-eye contact, so the next time you're on a date, and find your eye wandering to your phone every 5 minutes like one of Pavlov's dogs, ask yourself — *Who am I dating? This lovely woman, or my iPhone?* If you realize you want to date the woman, then show it by putting the phone away and making some consistent eye contact.

When it comes to the sending of junk pics or (ladies) pics of your luscious rack or milkshakified bootie, you can probably guess what Emily Post would say about those. *Just don't.* Trust me guys, no woman wants to see your dick wearing a mini-sombrero at 3am. And ladies, don't assume that boob shoot you just sexted, is going to just your beloved. Many of my straight male clients show their friends nudes pics of their girlfriends for bragging rights. "Hey check out my girlfriend's ___!" And many of my gay male clients, have Rolodexes of dick pics on their phones!

Don't think women are shy from sharing either. Soon that dick pic you were so proud of will be passed around your girlfriend's grandmother's bridge table and every octogenarian in the room will get a good look at your junk.

"Oh, look how much he has grown" ...And that's her granny talking (ouch).

Dating may seem like it's changed dramatically with the advent of new technology (and in many ways it has), but finding a love connection still comes down to knowing how to interact with people, and being present and courteous will never get stale. Unlike that dick pick that's being passed around right now. Sheesh, what were you thinking? A mini-sombrero? C'mon, man!

12 Just One More Thing — Be A Dating Detective

Unleash Your Inner Columbo To Verify Love's for Real

To avoid getting your feelings hurt in the modern dating game, you need to be on your toes. I'm not saying the single's pool is a cesspool of narcissists looking to use your body (it's not.) But to be safe, I encourage you to learn how to be a *dating detective* the next time you find yourself on a hot date or in a new relationship — why? So, you're fully aware of the actions and words of the person you may be swapping bodily fluids with for the rest of your life (or least a time or two). Back when I was a kid there was this TV show called *Columbo* where the main character was a disheveled detective (played by Peter Falk) who "roped a doped" people into thinking he was the worst detective ever, when really, he was playing them like a violin. Assuming Columbo was a simpleton, killers would drop their guards around him. Before you knew it, the people he was quietly investigating had confessed their crimes, without even realizing it.

You don't have to have a wrinkled raincoat or training from Scotland Yard to catch a bad boyfriend (or girlfriend) in the act. Lt. Columbo proved all you need to do is listen, so I encourage you to ask your hot new date questions, listen curiously, and watch for behavior patterns. You may find the words and actions of your hot date don't exactly add up. He or she may boast about having a certain skill or trait that doesn't jibe with what your eyes tell you. For example, they may claim they are "super open-minded" from traveling the world; but every time you suggest eating at an exotic restaurant, they resist like you were asking them to feast on chilled monkey brains.

Many of my clients have confided they tried to be a dating detective, but were so worried about how they would look on a date, they failed to notice the other person in detail. This is a very common thing; we all have self-conscious moments where it's extremely difficult to get out of our own heads, so we obsess over how we appear, or how we talk (mainly) to massage our own egos and prove to ourselves that we're as great as we think we are. Meanwhile, the other person floats by unexamined. How misguided is that? I realize it's not easy to multi-task on a date, but if you can find a way to turn that internal gaze outward, a little extra awareness and detective work can be your relationship savior.

Ask your inner Columbo: Do they seem as excited to be with you as you do with them? Have you noticed, every time you have great sex, he (or she) never calls the next day, or asks for another date in a normal time frame? Unleash your inner detective and you may find you are more into them, than they are you. What a downer, right? But at least you aren't fooling yourself. Coming to terms with the reality that you're not on the same wavelength as your future husband or wife hurts — but it's vital to having a healthy dating life. If your inner Columbo tells you that you've been pouring your heart into someone who doesn't feel the same way — it will suck royally to feel rejected, but you'll be glad you came to your senses. We all want to be adored, but as the song goes — *you can't make him love you if he won't.* Thanks Bonnie

Raitt for that hard-lyrical truth.

Falling head over heels in love can be the greatest feeling in the world. But sometimes it is perfectly healthy to step back from a hot and heavy romance with your detective hat on. Whatever you do, please do not follow the path of some people I know who have willingly and consciously gotten married to someone who doesn't love them.

Guess what? Those relationships *never last*.

The benefits of being a dating detective, even when it forces you to accept a painful truth is a healthy and necessary practice for dating, and frankly, for life.

Notice how you feel when you're with them.

Notice how you feel when you're without them.

Start doing this on the very first date. *Don't wait.* You will see patterns.

As much as you want to make excuses for him or her, don't dismiss warning signs as *"Oh, I'm just being neurotic."* That queasy way he or she makes you feel is probably how they make other people feel, too. So, don't sugar coat it. If you're unsure, let some friends in on what you discovered to get another opinion — because when many of my clients reflect back on their first dates with their exes — they kick themselves, because they saw red flags on their first date that would eventually be their relationship downfall. The truth was hiding in plain sight. And what do we do when we need some hidden truth revealed? Why, we conjure our inner Columbo to *crack the case...?*

13 Weeding Out Wackos, Weirdos, and Creeps

Avoid Dating on Islands Unless A Tribe's Got Your Back

Many singles today seem to have no trouble presenting themselves as confident, independent sex tigers on dating apps, but deep down, does anyone really want to date like a carnivorous loner with razor sharp teeth?

Wouldn't you rather date like a wise-eyed monkey instead?

As independent as we *think* we are, we humans are pack animals who crave validation and emotional support from our packs. Even if you're an agoraphobic nymphomaniac who's found a way to date while not leaving your house (I'm kind of impressed, *but still*) I feel we all could benefit from having a *Love Tribe* of trusted friends to help us filter out the wackos, weirdos, and creeps from the modern dating equation.

So why do many people still date like lone wolf sex tigers?

Clearly, people in love are not thinking straight!

The chemicals that hijack our brains when we're in love can be so darn potent — they can often (quite literally) blind us to reality. I liken it to being addicted to a powerful narcotic; we crave another hit from the love drug so effing bad — we don't bother questioning: Should I really be getting it from that Tinder dude with the Dracula avatar and the 1-800 number? That's a fair question for your love tribe (by the way), but far too often, it never even gets asked — what happened? Did our love tribes go extinct? Get bored? Get caught up with the Kardashians, or their own dating lives?

Everyone has different circumstances, but unless you met a group of trustworthy friends fairly early in life (usually when you were all single), I've found most of us tend to date on islands, for all kinds of reasons. The most obvious being — *hello*, new lovers don't want outsiders raining on their love parade; they just want to marinate in each other's (bonding) love hormones while humping their brains out, right? Who wants to go through a (possibly painful) introduction of a new partner to their friends, when they could be gazing into each other's eyes, planning a June wedding, or (yes) more humping?

Often, people will put off introducing their new lover to friends until the love drug has worn off a little. But by that time, the love attachment is already so strong that any negative reviews from friends will be taken as a personal insult. *Awkward* — right? Suddenly the new lover's defenses are up, and I've found it is almost impossible to penetrate someone's love bubble, even if a trusted friend is pointing out the obvious:

"He's so ambitious; isn't he? It's such a turn-on."

"Didn't he say he lives in a *camper van?*"

"You never support me in anything!"

See what I mean? Unless the trusted friend can convince the new lover, they are literally dating a serial killer, the love chemicals will almost always win out. Knowing all this: how can you avoid being blind-sided by some sexy stranger with strong pheromones in your own life? That's easy: find a *trustworthy tribe*. They will not only help you be a more *whole* person, they will also help introduce you to more people, and experiences. Our tribes refuel us when we feel empty, and they can save us when we get in too deep — and it's always nice to have a consulting team behind you when you're in need of a new life strategy, a gentle push into blind dating, or a complete dating reorg.

Don't tell anybody (OK, tell) but I've needed all three at some point in my life, and looking back, my tribe was vital to my success every time. I know some people who've gone so far as to reverse-engineer their love lives by (first) focusing on building their own community before starting to seriously look for *the one*. They told me, in the process, "Who knows what will happen?"

Whatever it takes for you to find your tribe, I encourage you to do it sooner rather than later, so the next time you start falling for some hot thing you barely know, you can consult with an objective mind, separate from your own, and get the opinion of somebody who's not marinating in your love chemicals. Don't push it off. Let your tribe in early on your *entire vetting process*. A group of friends (or even one reliable sounding board) can help validate your feelings, and ease any whispers of doubt you may have.

Now, let me just say: how you choose your tribe really matters, almost as much as how you choose a new lover. Your couch surfing college pal with 3 ex-wives will probably not be as full of sound relationship advice as (say) your well-adjusted roommate with the great fiancée you wish you were marrying. I would avoid relying on people like your beloved grandmother for dating advice because Granny has an ulterior motive (she just wants grandkids, dammit.) When taking any advice, always remember who your source is, and of course, trust yourself in the end. And when the time comes to introduce your new lover? Don't get cold feet!

You may be pleasantly surprised at how approving they are …

Here's a good example of what I mean.

A friend of mine (Amanda) was dating this new man (Sam) for about a month. She enjoyed his company but did not find him super attractive physically, but he was such a gentle, caring soul, she overlooked it because she thought he was interesting and easy to get along with. Amanda wanted to keep dating Sam but privately questioned her judgment, due to a string of bad relationships. Around that time, her two siblings came into town and wanted to meet Sam. Amanda was pretty nervous about introducing Sam to them but she had no choice! It didn't help that her best friend (Kelly) had recently run into Sam in the city and reported mixed first impressions.

With all these doubts swirling, Amanda was a tad on edge (to say the least) when her siblings, and her best friend, finally got to meet Sam one night at a restaurant.

Did Amanda's judgmental firing squad unleash their fury on poor Sam?

Actually, it was just the opposite.

Their dinner ended up being an *absolute blast*.

Sam was lighthearted, polite, and clicked with everyone. With the new approval of her trusted crew, Amanda's heart opened, and their love grew deeper. She told me, *"I owe a lot to that one dinner. Seeing them approve of Sam validated what I saw, and they even pointed out some good things about him that I'd never even thought about."*

I only mention this story to ease your trepidation about letting your friends in on your dating life. You won't always get this result, but I feel like it illustrates the benefits of dating out in the open, and not in the dark. If you trust your friends, and you like your new lover, let your community know it. If your friends are honest, and (this is beyond huge) — *you are actually open to receiving constructive feedback from them* — your tribe can help give you 20/20 vision throughout the entire dating process, and save you a lot of heartache by helping you to weed out the wack jobs or — like in Amanda's case — help you see the sparkling gem that is shining right in front of you.

14 So You Met Someone Amazing?

Timeless Dating Tips for The Modern Digital Age

We are all busy people with ridiculously overbooked lives. I get it. Some of you may be speed dating while reading this, for all I know, so I won't keep you — but the next time you have a date with someone so *gaga* great you find yourself stumbling over words while attempting to (gracefully as possible) suck down an appetizer of (highly-suggestive) bone marrow — I created this handy checklist to keep you from having an itchy gag reflex, due to nerves. Not that I think you need a *Cliff's Notes* on how to date — but if you're anywhere close to a social introvert (like me), your mind may suddenly go blank over the 2nd course. If (and when) it does, don't run to the bathroom to vomit. I encourage you to simply take a deep breath and reference these timeless dating tips in times of great doubt, awe, or butterfly-induced nausea. If you do, I'm confident you will put your best foot forward (and not in your mouth) and live to date another day. Here we go my horny little pretties ... repeat after me:

1. **Talk Less & Listen More** — Actively listening is always a great first move on a date. In a world full of people

who love to talk about themselves, listening can be one of the sexiest ways to impress a date. Listen closely to the things they say like: how they view relationships, or why they date, at all. Try to detect some behavior patterns while you're at it — be a dating detective. Are they negative, self-centered, respectful of others, difficult to plan a date with? Resist the urge to convince yourself they are more "into you" than they are. If they say they're not interested in relationships, *believe them & move on*. Unless you're into that sort of thing, then, by all means, *bone away*.

2. Show Genuine Interest — People can't help but feel close and connected to people who show genuine interest in them. So, ask questions and really care, you can't fake it! Pay attention, be present — let your date feel your attention basking over them, because genuine interest and caring are building blocks to emotional intimacy. I don't want to give you shortcuts to appearing genuine (that in itself would be insincere) but if you ever get stuck, an old therapist's trick is to reflect back on what you just heard them say, like, *"It sounds like you really want to travel abroad next year."* And *"Wow, that's interesting, tell me more"* never kills a conversation. It confirms you're listening and keeps someone talking, and *always keep them talking*. You might find what you thought was a finished subject can go way deeper than you ever imagined.

3. Have Fun with It — This goes for a first date or for 20 years of marriage; laughter and a warm smile opens people up, and creates a feeling of safety between partners. Plus, it's healthy for you to smile. Most single people are out to have fun on dates, so tell them you're having fun, and show it on your face. Even if the date sucks, but you like the person

— *make it fun.* I knew a woman who mildly cut her hand during a date; instead of going home, they went to the store together to find bandages. While searching the aisles, she playfully tossed him a box of Depends, and said, *"For your leaking."* It was a bold move, but he busted out laughing, replying loudly, *"Did you find your ringworm medicine yet?"* What could have been a lousy date ended up being really memorable because they both had fun with it. So, have fun, it's what dating is all about!

4. Have Some Manners, Will Ya? — Take the time to plan a date with confidence and be flexible if plans go sideways. If they hate seafood — maybe don't take them to an all-you-can-eat shrimp night at the fish grotto? Cater to your date's wishes, not your idea of what they want. This may sound old fashioned, but try to keep your date PG in the beginning. This shows you're not an animal (who was raised in a barn) and you've got some class. It can also add a little mystery and perhaps some sexual tension to the mix, which is always nice when that itch is eventually scratched, right?

5. Forget Your Past Lovers — I know it still hurts at times, but I encourage you not to bring your past failed relationships into new ones. Talk about a romance killer. There's nothing less sexy than dating someone who demands you to love them, but is so bitter from a past breakup, they no longer believe in love themselves. Don't be that jaded person; I don't care how hot you look brooding with your shirt off. Your mindset matters so please, do not go on a new date with a closed-off mentally. Believe me, it will show. Do your best to let go of old bruises from years ago or they may psych you out of finding a new love *right now.* If you're not there yet, that's OK. You may have some healing to do before you upload that dating app photo …

6. Beware of Power Trippers — The good news is they're fairly easy to spot. The bad news is you may be on a date with one! Maybe it begins with a comment about your outfit being "less than," which can soon escalate to, *"I don't think you should hang out with Sharon anymore,"* or *"You should stop doing* (fill in the blank). Listen to how your date orders food. Observe how they treat your server. Take note of how they treat you.

Do they deflect responsibility? Do they have chauvinistic tendencies? Do you sense whiffs of narcissism? If you see red flags, they will only get bigger as a relationship goes on. Your lover may even "have your best interests" in mind, but it doesn't mean they can control you. Power trippers have the tendency to become abusers, and no one (full stop) should stand for abusive behavior. I suggest you avoid power trippers like the plague.

7. Leave Your Beer Goggles at Home — If you love waking up with your underwear missing and fuzzy (to no) memories of the night before — drinking too much on a date is a sure-fire way to get there! I'm no teetotaler, but please, watch the booze intake around new dates. Getting hammered on a first date is like playing the human version of pin-the-tail-on-the-donkey with your sexy bits. It may feel like all those tequila shots were necessary to ease your social anxiety (and they may do the trick for a while). But in the morning, the odds are pretty good you will wake up in a strange spinning bed, with a person you barely recognize, and wish to God you had that blindfold back.

8. Be Honest & Always Be Yourself — In the end, they may not *love us like we could have loved them* — but one thing we can do is be transparent and honest about our intentions, and our selves. Why make up a fictional "tech billionaire" persona when it's just going to lead to disappointment? If you're "just not into them" then just say it (in a nice way, of course), and let the other person deal with reality. I've found your love karma will stay intact if you don't lead people on, and are honest. Then (at least) you can say you tried your best and (simply) hope the universe meets you halfway with a love connection that is as genuine as you are. That's really all you can do, karma wise.

15 As the Loins Turn

Let's Talk About Sex, Baby!

Do you ever feel like Neo from The Matrix when you have sex — like someone was offering you a perception-altering, orgasm-inducing pill that might melt your brain forever? Am I the only one? If you just answered, "Uh nooo, sex is sex," fair enough, but I encourage you to keep an open mind because, to some people, sex can be like the *naked Matrix*, and to others, it can be a truly *Kafkaesque experience*. Despite the standard way most movies and TV still portray "making love" — the act of sex can be a profoundly different experience for people. What you believed was a healthy romp in the hay, could be another person's sacred act of lovemaking.

How can we ever know what our lovers are truly thinking?

Unless we can read minds, we can't, really. A friend once got a fortune cookie that read, *"Each Head Is A World of Its Own"* — I love that proverb because it's so true when it comes to sex. You just never know what your partner is thinking, which leads me to a topic that I know some people will not want to hear — don't judge. *Believe me,* my European mother (a middle school sex education teacher) raised me to be very open about sex, so I'm absolutely, positively, sex-positive — I love sex, I really do.

But now that I've said that, I want you to hear me when I say

— if you really like that new guy you've been going on about, and you want him to stick around, I gently encourage you to *resist the urge to have sex* on the first date — or the 2nd or maybe even the 8th date for that matter. What, no sex? What kind of dating book is this??

In case I just lost half my audience — let me be clear, I'm not saying hold out until marriage! I'm merely suggesting you delay hitting up the bone zone a bit longer than your libido says is reasonable.

Besides, if you really think you may have found "the one" — holding out a little longer will allow you to not blur your decision-making with all those warm and fuzzy attachment sex hormones. Great sex can cause some us to miss warning signs because the sex was so freaking good, they spent more time with their eyes rolled in the back of their heads, rather than looking for red flags.

I'm not suggesting you *play mind games* with your lovers. *Hmm, no thank you. Authenticity, honesty, and kindness* can be their own powerful aphrodisiacs, *seriously!* Try holding back those eager beavers and wild horses a little while longer; I know delayed gratification isn't for everyone, all I'm saying is it may make sense for you to resist jumping into bed with your latest "Mr. or Ms. Right" if you truly want a future with them. Because once you give up *that booty* (whatever yours may look like) — you are rolling the dice with the power dynamic. Just know you are gambling.

That beautiful creature you slept with last night may not return your texts so quickly today. Maybe you already feel connected to them while they don't feel like responding? Or the roles are reversed and you're less interested because you just hit that last night? Now, last night's fun feels like an obligation; suddenly, things have changed. See how it works? You just never know how someone will feel after sex; especially if you (ahem) do not know them very well. Unless you're training to be a triathlete at the next Sex Olympics, I encourage you to resist riding the hobbyhorse until you know you want to be entangled with your new lover physically, emotionally, and *with expectations*. Because if you stick around long enough, they're coming, whether you like it or not ...

Now, I will say, in some situations, casual sex can have its benefits, more than enough, in fact, for some people. These are what I call transactional "sex taxi" relationships that just get you to the next relationship. If you're a heavy user of sex taxis, I would suggest you ask yourself — *What am I getting out of this? Great sex? Validation I'm sexy? A distraction from pain? Am I filling an insecurity? Am I exploring my sexual orientation?* Whatever your reasons, watch out for hurt feelings — because these things called "postcoital emotions" can happen after sex — even in a sex taxi.

And if all that hot sex ever leaves you cold at night, wondering, "What's it all about?" Maybe consider shaking up the way you approach your next sexual opportunity? Maybe even resist serving up another hot slice of *that booty* until you know it's for real?

It just might shake up your outcomes, too ...

16 The Booty Call Rorschach Test
What Does Sex Even Mean to You?

Yes, my horny little pretties, how we perceive the act of sex or (*making sweet love*) is very individualized experience that is often layered with unrealistic expectations from (at least) one of the participants. I've even had clients tell me they truly believed the *sex worker* they recently hired was really into them. Whaaa?

When I asked, "Why do you feel that way?"

He said, *"Because we talk a lot after sex, and she loves the way I touch her."*

I explained to him that, sure, the sex worker might be "into" him, but I had counseled quite a few in my career, so the more likely explanation was he had simply forgotten that he hired a sex worker to fulfill this fantasy.

My client hadn't considered the possibility that "pillow talk" was also included in the price. The closeness he felt after sex had blinded him to this (fairly) obvious fact. So, yes, in case you were wondering — men can also have post coital love attachments, too. I only mention this story to show you how feelings can get twisted up into strange sexual pretzels once coitus is introduced into any relationship, *even when you have a straightforward contract with a sex worker.*

Not to put you on the spot, but since sex can be so mysterious and deeply personal, in order to understand the sexual baggage that you will be bringing to your next relationship (and you are bringing sexual baggage, we all are), I feel it's productive if you took some time to non-judgmentally explore *what sex even means to you?* Are you numb to it? Bored by it? Scared of it? Compulsively addicted? Not to drop *too much information* on you but I've had clients tell me they masturbate until their genitals bleed, while others have admitted they dread sex, and will only have it in the dark with a shirt on, when they feel they can't turn down their partner, yet again.

If this question has never crossed your mind, give it some thought! And if you're a straight man, I gently urge you to understand that your partner's feelings after sex is quite different than your post-sex feeling, due to the hormone's women release after sex. So, if your answer to the question, "What sex means to you?" is you tend to treat it like a sport? Please be sensitive to your partner, and (please) don't be a douchebag dater.

If you feel sex is strictly physical (and not emotional), it might be a good exercise to pinpoint where that feeling started. Not that it's right or wrong — but were you a late bloomer? Were you picked on at school? Did someone you love reject you in your formative years? Be honest. You may discover your reason for being a "Pick Up Artist" (sorry that was uncalled for) may not be related to any of the examples I just offered. But whatever your backstory, I hope you will try to work through any past traumas you uncover that may be influencing your "sex as sport" lifestyle. Try to think back to what messages (if any) your parents, past partners, or even your religion taught you about sex, and how they helped form your views.

I know it may seem pointless to dredge up old memories,

especially if you have no past traumas in your closet — but I feel like it could be a very healthy exercise for you in your dating life, no matter what sex, ultimately, means to you. Uncovering your core motivations for why you have sex the way you do, can be a liberating feeling (and guess what, it can make you an even better lover!) So, I encourage you to explore yourself whenever you get the chance, with gusto. Hopefully, not until your sexy bits bleed, *yikes*.

17 He May Not Be Perfect, But Is He Perfect for You?

Evolving from Honeymoon Bliss into An Even Higher Love

We all want to live in the throes of passionate love; no one wants to see those hot embers go out. We all seem to yearn to find our perfect mate and then dream of living in that honeymoon phase, forever on an endless loop of great sex ... Hey, I want to look 21 forever with a surfer/model body while still eating my daily dose of ice cream — but guess what? Change is inevitable in life. Sadly, that honeymoon phase will end one day for all lovers — but it doesn't mean true love has to end with it.

As much as our youth-crazy culture is obsessed with chasing that honeymoon feeling, over the cliff if necessary (see every Bachelor show, ever) — as I get a little wiser, the more I realize how few people today realize *there is a second life to lasting love.* All that passionate sex you were having in the beginning of your romance, can actually evolve into an even deeper, more fulfilling love that's (maybe) less sex-tastic, but chock full of all kinds of mutual respect and love for one another, even after *all flaws have been exposed.* That's a pretty neat trick, right?

But can someone really still love a person after they know all their flaws? Despite what our society tells us, I think so (see every old couple, ever!) My grandfather once told me, "True love is what happens when the honeymoon is over. When you finally see all their flaws, and you still deeply care for them? That's true love, right there."

Not to bag on Millennials, but I've observed a lot of young people today seem to assume that once the hot sex phase is over, it's time to find another mate. How did this belief get started? Is it because our culture loves *disposable everything*? Is it because our media doesn't spend much time promoting the many benefits of "getting busy while getting old?" I can see how that visual would not be all that sexy on a 50-inch HDTV...

Whatever the reason for the misconception, I believe there is something profoundly awesome about sticking with your mate for life, and letting your mutual love evolve into something much more powerful. You see, once the honeymoon is through, all those layers of identity we wear to protect us, come tumbling down (on both sides). So now, lovers finally get to see the real person they've been having sex with. What you thought was the absolutely perfect man with absolutely perfect abs — turns out to be a flawed human with a gut, after all. That's actually a good thing!

If you ever get to this stage in a relationship, I'm telling you, you're doing great. But now you both have to dig deep and ask yourselves, "Without the love drug blinding me — do I still deeply love that flawed idiot?" Can you believe, some of the happiest people around say, "Oh yeah, look at those flaws, they're gorgeous!"

As for what's better: chasing hot passion forever, or easing into lasting love? I wish I had the universal answer; every relationship is its own unique animal. But if (years from now) after you and your mate have gotten past the honeymoon phase, and you look up and realize (holy crap) my entire glorified image of my lover has been cracked wide open. You'll have to ask yourself the million-dollar questions:

Can I still love this flawed person?

Does sticking around for the laid back "after party" feel like settling?

Do I secretly still yearn for him to be someone that he isn't?

Am I only staying because it's easy, and I don't want to be alone?

These are all tough questions, but I've found when people cite "ease of use" as a big relationship plus, to take note. If you are in an "easy" relationship, you have to decide — Does it mean I'm settling, or does it mean we are just really compatible? Maybe you will discover that easy breezy feeling you get (just being around him) is the result of most of your ideals actually being met?? What a concept, eh?

Sometimes dreams can come true, even after the hot sex party has ended. You may not feel forever "high on the love drug" after the honeymoon phase ends, but you can take comfort in the fact you feel immensely satisfied in a solid, loving, and symbiotic relationship that lasts a lifetime. Don't just take it from me; listen to yourself. If your gut tells you that loving this flawed, yet highly loveable person is a good fit — I'd probably take that advice. That's not settling — that's *true love*, baby.

18 Earth to You, What Were You Thinking?

When Sex Is Out of This World, Beware of Fogged Helmet Syndrome

Mind-blowing sex can be a tingly, sometimes deceiving, gift from the libido Gods, particularly when you haven't had sex in a while. When it's soo good, it's soo hard to pass up, ooooh, I get it. But if you're looking for someone special to spend your life with, hooking up with an Olympic-level sex decathlete can be a distracting setback.

Can a mind-blowing sex partner ever become a long-lasting soul mate?

Sometimes, ABSOLUTELY, but I wouldn't bet my lifelong happiness on it. Generally, rock star sex partners are what we think they are: super passionate, great in bed, devilishly charming — but they're not always the most reliable people you'll ever meet when the sun comes up! But how would you know you're dating a sexy jerk if you're combing your bed-head out all the time? Mind-blowing sex has a sneaky way of steaming up your hormonal headlights, and bonding incompatible lovers by flooding their erogenous zones with love hormones, which can hide a lot of your sexy partner's character flaws, for weeks, months, even years. Not only that, all that "O juice" rushing through your loins

MASTER DATER

can actually trick you into thinking you LOVE your sexual dynamo, *even if you barely know the dude.*

Let's say you have a friend who met someone special. They tell you, *"I've met the one! It's like porn star sex with her! Check out this pic she sent!"* Maybe your friend thinks his new girlfriend is a bit odd and introverted, but who cares when the sex is banging? This couple will likely fool themselves into thinking they're in a pretty good relationship simply because of their great sexual connection. But once the sex-train slows down (and it often does) your friend may realize that going to the DMV, or getting a root canal is more fun than having a conversation with his sexy lover! But since their coitus was like Caligula on nitrous oxide, your friend missed all the warning signs.

We all probably know a person who ended up with a partner who's not in their same league. But they stay together, far longer than they should; hmm, what invisible force is keeping these poorly matched lovers in the same bed? There may be many reasons (money, kids, mutual friends), but it could be because they have great sex! This type of confusion (between body, mind, and soul) can lead people to hitch their wagons to sexy disasters, over and over again.

Some people who chase the Big O like their own personal White Whale will even use a persuasive form of mental gymnastics to justify dating their sexy, flawed lovers. They'll say things like, *"I don't think he's nice, really, but we've been having lots of sex — so I feel I should try to see this through, or I'll feel like a slut."* This is how many unhappy couples are created. The truth is unless you've discussed the matter, you probably don't have a loving, or even an emotionally committed, relationship with your hot new lover, even though your post-sex hormones (may) say otherwise.

So, you can't trust your loins OR your heart when you're dating a rock star lover? Um, *not really*. They'll tell you anything just to keep those love hormones coming!

Now, if you really LOOOOVE what your sex tiger does for you, and your goal is simply to get laid, then own it, and be proud. I'm not saying all casual sex is bad, but if you demand your coitus be hot, and served twice daily, and you still think you're on some holy hunt to find "the one" — you may be deluding yourself. I'm not saying you are — but *you kinda are*. Because when the smoke clears on your waterbed, and the coconut-oiled sheets have been washed (or burned), you may realize you failed to notice a barrage of red flags, or detect any behavior patterns about your "hunka-hunka" burning love. If you're using mind-blowing sex as the sole determining factor in your love equation, you may end up wasting years of your life kicking the tires on every bad boy and sex goddess that comes your way. And believe me, it's never fun to realize your sexy partner totally lacks compassion, or empathy, or a freaking soul!

If you suspect your loins and heart are conspiring against you — you have to find a quiet moment when you're not getting freaky to ask yourself, *"Do I really love this insensitive sex machine, or do I just love what he does for me?"*

If you're kicking yourself because (you want to fall in love) but you just realized you're only in your current relationship for the hot sex, then consider the alternative: Would you sacrifice some of that porn star-loving to have a better-quality soul mate? If you answered, "Yes!" I encourage you to zip up, and keep looking, because all that great sex you're having with that random "sex taxi operator" is probably standing in the way of you finding your soul mate.

The role sex plays in relationships is so vital, yet so different for everyone — but if that's all you're chasing? Then own it, babe.

But know that it can warp your perspective and complicate your entire freaking life! Think of sex as being 10%-20% part of your future relationship. Sooo scratch that itch if you feel like it, my horny pretties. Just know that a sexy lover can distract even the best dating detectives from their real goal. Do you even remember your dating goal?

Wipe that fog off your helmet!

19 Sexual Purrfection

Tantalizing Tips That Will Keep Her Purring All Night

L ike all the Tinder couples who say, "Screw the whole courtship thing. Let's be F-buddies, stranger." I want to fast forward at warp speed to when you both choose to let your naughty bits fly. I never relish making general statements about the opposite sex (so get ready guys!) But it seems that a lot of men today (not all) have gotten misguide info on sex tips! Have you noticed that you rarely hear us talking about sensuality anymore, or how they get off by making their partner feel incredible, anymore? Wouldn't it be awesome if we did?

Where has all the seduction gone, and how can we get it back? Because that's what many women want, guys. When it comes to pleasing a woman in the bedroom — please, do us all a favor, and put down the porn and the lube, and break out the rose water, and the roses, for that matter. Before you even think about penetration, there is this thing called "wooing" you need to master first, or at least attempt, if you want to hook up with the woman of your wet-dreams.

The next time you meet a lady you really like, put your bat on the bench for a while, and see if you can unlock her mind before attempting to unlock her chastity belt. Because as much as bro culture likes to wish it were true, for women, sex is not an X-game to be conquered with a sweet power move. Most women I know dream of meeting a man who will give us a romantic and sensual sexual odyssey that lasts three days.

Or at least 3 minutes! Ugh, for some women it's come to that.

Your special woman may not say it out loud (to you, at least) so let me do it for them: if you want to make your sex kitten purr in the sack, you have to forget about yourself for a hot minute, and focus on giving her a highly-sensual, extremely personal lovemaking *experience*. Yes, I said experience. Not a quickie, or a bang sesh. An experience! So forget about hitting, tapping, or banging that ass (guys), and start thinking about charming that ass, wooing it, teasing it, seducing it — *becoming one with it.*

To prime her erotic pump, so to speak, they should think of the entire date night as foreplay for the bedroom because that is what your lady friend is thinking. Cease the incessant chatter about work, politics, or yourself over dinner, and start listening to her.

Be genuine. Be present. Be selfless.

Focus on her entirely. I know that may sound obvious, but you'd be surprised how myopically dense some us can be when sex is a possibility. You can't just show up and expect to get laid. Throw some woo! Make her feel beautiful with sincere, detailed compliments about her as a person. You may also compliment her appearance, but don't objectify her. Many women feel like their bodies are just vehicles for another person's pleasure, so find a minute to let her know that your needs are not what's important right now. Tonight, it's all about her ...

When you finally get her in the bedroom, pay close attention to what she likes. Tell her, *"I want to explore every part of you."* Then do it, and take it slow. Warm her up. Did you know love hormones are exchanged with extending, open mouthed-kissing? Give it a try, guys! It's fun and will help turn her engine on.

It's OK if it takes some time for her flower to bloom, she may not be used to all the attention you're giving her. Don't get frustrated, keep the sensuality coming. Spend time playing, massaging, exploring. Think of her pleasure as a special puzzle for you to solve, so be intuitive. Relaxing her is a must, before you can unleash her inner sex tigress, so find the spots in her body that (when kissed, touched, or licked) lift her hips off the bed, wanting more. An arched back is a great clue that you're on the right track. Another indicator is when she paws aggressively for you to "Don't stop!"

If you hear those magic words, keep going! She's close to purring.

Did you know most women actually get more pleasure from (hand or vibrator) genital stimulation than they do from the actual D? It's true. Sorry gentlemen, your junk alone is not our magic bullet orgasm cure! We can actually get there much faster (on our own) with our handy-dandy bullet vibrator. I know that may sting, but some women can take the penis, or leave it — so wield yours only when she asks. And if you're going to stick anything inside of her (whatever it is) I suggest you not jam it up her vagina like a power tool! If you're using a vibrator, a hand or a tongue, work around the outside of the V, and find the little man in the boat. You know what that is, right?

For your woman's sake, *I hope so.*

If she offers to give you oral sex, hey, go ahead, and accept her generous gift.

But don't pressure her for a blowjob, and never push her head down to your crotch, that never works, and is extremely demeaning! Every woman's sexuality is its own mosaic — so listen to her, talk to her, and observe how her body reacts to your touch. A good rule is, if you can tell she's into it, don't change positions, keep doing exactly what you're doing! There's no need to jump around to other moves, which may surprise men who like to change sex positions like they're contortionists at Cirque Du Soleil for their own visual stimulation. Do you acrobatic guys know that all of those position changes can actually slow down a women's build up to O heaven? SOOO, if you already have her howling at the moon, *take the hint.* Let her close her eyes and focus on herself — encourage her to do it. Remember, you're tending to her garden of love, not your power steering pump! Did you know it's even possible to give her multiple orgasms through something I call "next level cunnilingus?" You must get consent before you try it, but if she gives you the green light to push past her initial post-orgasm squirmy stage, to go for the BIG ONE — you probably won't have to go to town much longer until she hit rolling O train that could wake your neighbors and go down in the history books, as well as earn you more than a few gold stars … just saying!

And if you happen to work her fertile soil for hours until your lips and tongue are beyond numb, hey, you did your best. It is every woman's responsibility for their own orgasm, so don't sulk if you work and work, and still no O. You can always try again tomorrow! *Or in an hour or two.*

After you shower all this attention on her, don't worry, you'll still get your turn! Your equipment will still work, so don't rush it. You can even do a little experiment and see if giving her pleasure actually turns you on. It works for lots of men … Come on, it's not that hard to be selfless in bed! Being a caring and attentive sex partner comes back to being a whole person. Whole people may not be flashy rock stars in bed, but they tend to make excellent, and attentive sex partners. To make yourself more "whole" (see Chapter 8), I encourage you to work on understanding your sexuality.

If you want to be a better sex partner, don't just focus on her. Find out what you like. Don't be shy. Work through any shameful feelings you may have been conditioned to have about your sexuality, and throw all those puritanical hang-ups away, because all that stuff is outdated anyway. It may not be easy to shed whatever hang-ups you may have overnight. It will take time, but most of us shy away from even trying to understand what turns us on and why, so try already! Remember, it's your pleasure too …

When you aren't some oiled-up sex machine, I hope you will find some quiet time to work on feeling "whole" enough that you can say (to yourself and your partner) you know what? I deserve pleasure, too. Sex is never about just pleasing another person. You also have to love yourself, too. So, men, if you want to live out that (non-porn) yet still super-hot fantasy you keep dreaming about, the more comfortable you are with yourself, the more comfortable your partner will be, and the more your sex life can grow.

I said grow, not shrink!

20 He's Gonna Blooow!

How to Get Him Eating Out of the Palm of your Hand

When it comes to pleasuring men and their, let's face it, easy-to-operate junk, you can fall into the trap of assuming that all men should be easy to please, because often times, they are! But let's not phone in a "C" performance in the bedroom, we're all adults here. I feel like we all can raise our sex games, so I encourage you to keep raising yours even when it seems like your beaux, boo, or bae just needs a few basic sex moves to make him happy. Remember, men are visual creatures, so if you want to lure your man into some next level sex-capades, I suggest you set the scene by presenting yourself like a package for him to unwrap. Try to groom, shave, and pluck all the appropriate areas, so you look like you put some effort into it. Should you buy lingerie for your man? I say, absolutely, go all Agent Provocateur on him if it makes you feel sexy, *but you don't have to.* What about leather? If that makes you feel hot, unleash your inner BDSM sex goddess. *But you don't have to.* I've also found completely nude works pretty great, too!

On your hot date, the goal is to make him feel seen and heard. If you're on your first date, don't be afraid to touch his arm or shoulder, fairly early in the evening. It can be a nice little icebreaker that will make him feel wanted and comfortable. Go ahead, flirt, tease, be playful, if it's in your nature. Let your man know that you're happy, and feeling sexy tonight. If he's not sure of it, make it crystal clear that you're really into him.

I've noticed that some us are so in their own heads that they miss this very basic move. When it finally comes time to make sweet-sweet love, think about undressing slowly for him, and letting him take in all your sexiness. Take it slooow. What's the rush? Maybe try a tiny little striptease, or let him slowly underdress you? Or you can always slowly undress him, too. Whatever feels right, do it! As much as you may desperately want to turn off the lights before sex, men love the visual stimulation, so keep the lights on, if you can stand it. You can even watch some porn with him with ridiculous names like *"How Harry Ate Sally"* but don't demean yourself, or agree to anything that makes you uncomfortable.

If you're dating a man over 30 — don't expect him to sprout an insta-boner like a teenage boy the moment you unbuckle his belt. Some men take longer to rise to the occasion, especially if you just had cocktails with a guy over 50! Some men will be ready to go in 2.2 seconds, while others can have a slight case of stage fright. Whatever reveals itself to you (or not) just cool your expectations a bit, and give it some time to develop as you play together, and learn what turns each other on. An extended foreplay session will help you figure out how to best get his blood flowing down there. His whole body is obviously fair game here, but let's be honest, his D is probably where he wants you to focus! My guess is the vast majority of men would much rather get a blowjob over a handjob since I feel like men can give themselves hand jobs on their own, much better than anyone else can do for them, right? Not to rule out hand jobs as a good foreplay move. I don't want to take anything off the table, especially if you're not into giving oral.

Some foreplay is better than nothing.

As a teenager, I giggled over bananas and cucumbers (I'm an equal opportunity food perverter). I wondered, how do I blow job this thing?

Deep breath and what? Blow out candles?

So here are my old lady cougar suggestions that will have him begging for more. If you're dating a guy over 30, guess what? He doesn't have to be rock hard to start performing. Ever hear of a fluffer? If not Google it. Your lips can be like a snake charmer to his love muscle. Variety is key in fellatio, so mix up your moves. A strong use of your tongue up and down his shaft never hurts. Whatever you do, keep your teeth out of it! A little teasing can be great, as well as a lot of eye contact (guys love that). I've also found some hot and heavy breathing over a wrecked penis can make men go wild. And don't forget, your hands should always be working in conjunction with your mouth. If you're using lubricant, feel free give his love pump a gift by mixing in a slight twisting motion to the typical "up and down" hand stimulation to give him even more sensation. And don't forget the ugly stepchildren, the balls, which should be gently caressed and handled, especially right before he pops.

One of the biggest misconceptions about oral sex, is you have to deep throat the D to be incredible. *Not true.* I always say a firm, but not too tight, hold at the base of his shaft, plus some consistent suction from your lips, usually works just fine. Watch and feel his body to find a rhythm while you do it. But if you are genuinely curious about deep throating — it's not always a power play from some porn-obsessed bro. It can actually be pleasurable for the woman, and can really send a man spinning! Even if you do it for just a short time, for some men, it's a sure-fire way to get him from semi-erect to hard. And if you do have an itchy gag reflex, but still want to try oral, try popping in a menthol cough drop before heading south. It thickens your salvia to make the process easier, and even adds a little "snow job" tingle factor for him. I realize this may seem like a lot of work, but trust me, feeling him be SOO pleased with your bedroom skills can be really fun for you, too.

But, once you have "done" him, will he "do" you?

It's the eternal question, right?

How are we still having this conversation?

I have no idea, but I get a bit turned off by the double-standard of men who demand oral, but don't return the favor. If, after you perform, you're dying for your man to go down on you, and he doesn't? Gently explain to him what you want. Remind yourself that your pleasure if important too. If you don't want to call him out, perhaps casually mention that you've found some people who offer to perform oral, are (cough cough) subliminally showing their partner what they hope to receive in return — women, in particular. Maybe the humor will open up the discussion. But don't stuff your desires and the communication under the bed, so to speak. I totally get that not everyone is game for oral sex, and that's fine. I don't want to pressure anyone (man or woman) to do anything they don't want to do. Just don't let them shame you for not being an oral queen, especially if he doesn't return the favor. There should absolutely be no jamming heads in crotches. That's a deal-breaker.

Now, if you ladies want to play with the rest of his body during foreplay, go ahead — it's an extra bonus for him. If you really pay attention, and mix up your foreplay moves with lots of variety, you'll know what turns him on by his body's reaction to your sexual repertoire. Once you have your man begging for sex — then …

This is as far as my foreplay refresher course goes!

What you do next is up to you. But never forget, ladies, the sexiness you feel inside of you can fill an entire (small) planet. It can be a huge turn-on for men to see that you're getting genuine pleasure from pleasuring him, so do your best to own your sexuality, and have some fun! Always keep open lines of communicate with your man, and always practice safe sex. Remember, your personal ethics translates to the bedroom too, so if there's ever any question about what turns you (or your partner) on, I encourage you to openly talk about what both of your sexual needs are.

If you're a bit shy, you can always share a sexy video or GIF of a position you want to try. Ahem, rumor has it some people are sharing clips from (lady friendly) Tumblr sites with their sex partners (rather than telling them what they want). I say, whatever works! Whether you're into performing fellatio or not, giving hand jobs or not, watching porn or not, wearing leather or not, all of our bodies can be John Mayer wonderlands with lots of fun equipment to play with, so go enjoy your wonderland of flesh, and try to give your hunk some pleasure along the way, so you're making the best of your sexy Motherf**er years (as Prince so eloquently put it.) I say, try every ride in your partner's wonderland once. Some way-way *more than once!*

21 Seasoned Coitus: A Dish Best Served Old?

Experience Can Be Super Sexy; I'm Serious!

Ageism is (sadly) rampant in our culture, but especially in the modern dating game. The old dude with the pointy, overgrown gray eyebrows you see doing grandpa yoga in the park, or the matronly woman with the sensible floral top who speed waddles around your neighborhood every morning, are not exactly the definition of sexy in our youth-obsessed culture. Today, older single people are often written-off as sexual lepers, but you'd be shocked if you knew how often your grandparents were getting their freaks on! You may have just gagged a bit there because we've all been conditioned to believe the idea of old people having sex is a major turn-off, but, guess what? *You will get old one day, too.*

Don't you want to have someone to love, even when your naughty bits are old enough to collect Social Security? No matter how you feel about your grandparents bumping geriatric uglies, I invite you to reconsider the power of *seasoned coitus*. I'm telling you, it can be fantastically satisfying, which should give us all hope that our sex lives won't die when we hit retirement age, because it *never should.*

Sure, when you get older, your equipment doesn't work exactly the same, after having children (for women) and lower testosterone (for men), it's only natural. But just because your junk is vintage doesn't mean you're less of a lover. I've heard many times how "experienced" lovers are often (surprisingly) good in bed. I know, that may not be the hottest visual you've ever had, but here me out! Think back to when you were having sex in high school or college. How much did you really know about pleasing your partners, or even yourself? Not much, right? That describes *all of us*.

That's why so many of our early sex memories are so painfully bad.

But what about now? I bet you've probably gained some wisdom in the bedroom over the years, right? Perhaps you've even put in your proverbial 10,000 hours in the bone-zone? Okay, maybe that's a tad optimistic for most people, but don't shortchange yourself. If you've been paying attention, and working on your sex game, you've almost certainly gathered lots of sensuality tips that have made you a better lover than you ever were in high school.

Another huge reason older people can be sneaky-sexy is because they're usually fully formed (whole) individuals who know exactly who they are, and what they want in life, and in the bedroom. Don't overlook how sexy it is to *know yourself* in all your rawness. Not only that, older people are often far better individuals than they were as horny young smart asses. There is something about getting older that makes us get our crap together and finally become kinder, gentler people as we age. Age also seem to give people the *courage to be vulnerable* in front of their partners, which can make their love connections, even more fulfilling.

So, if you ever find yourself horny and single as you reach retirement age, you don't have to buy a Japanese sex robot to grow old with (unless that's your kink). Just put on that Mumu, or those Bermuda Shorts, and don't forget the lube, or the Viagra when you make your debut on the senior's dating scene. It doesn't matter how much you're sagging, you still have plenty of miles on your sex odometer! Whomever you choose to be your romantic partner in your golden years, know that as you strut around looking hot in your orthopedic shoes, your character and wisdom, in and out of the bedroom, is what will lead you to the well-seasoned partner of your dreams.

And if you ever find that your sexual juices (or pup tent) aren't quite working like they once did, talk to your doctor about it. Prescription medication (not your body) is often the culprit. Before you have an awkward moment in bed — embrace that awkward moment with your doctor, when you tell them that you want to keep having sex until your equipment falls off. Trust me, the look on your doctor's face will be priceless!

22 Keeping Up with The Boneses
Your Sexual Education Should Never End in Junior High School

Remember that awkward Sex Ed. class we giggled our way through as kids? Unfortunately, for a lot of poor souls that was the only non-porn related sex education *they ever had.* Stunning, right? Is our country really that puritanical to gloss over our emerging sexualities with one class in junior high? Um — *yes, it is.* Are we nation full of sexually dysfunctional people? The jury is still out on that one, but I can tell you I've counseled countless individuals, usually women, who were shamed into subverting their sexual desires as teens by some hypocritical authority figure (often an older white man) who, no doubt, wasn't getting laid enough himself. Being the child of a sex education teacher, I empathize with anyone who had to sit through this type of sermon from a parent, teacher, or even worse, some perverted clergyman, because this type of adolescent brainwashing can affect the way we view sex for the rest of our lives.

If I just described you (I'm sorry you had to go through that) but here's the good news — you can continue your own sex education *right now*, no matter how old you are. If you feel inexplicable shame after masturbating or blush when you walk past a sex store, yet secretly wish you and your partner could keep up in the bedroom with your neighbors who love to flaunt their tantric sex *loudly* — just like getting to Carnegie Hall, all it takes is *practice, practice, practice*. My first suggestion to "keeping up with the boneses'" is one I tell all my clients — Take personal inventory before you sign up for that tantric sex class or go on a shopping spree at *Good Vibrations*. Because you need to face your own attitudes about sex, as well as any sexual traumas or hang-ups before you face off with someone new in bed.

Because we all have our flaws.

I certainly have my fair share, and I imagine you do as well. But don't think your personality quirks are hidden when you're buck naked: *they are probably only magnified.* If you are a control freak in life, your lover probably thinks you're the same way in bed. If you're an adventurous type person in your day-to-day, the odds are pretty good your lover thinks that you're a sex explorer in the sack.

Of course, there are exceptions to this rule. I've definitely met a few sex explorers who were just the opposite in their real life!

But whatever type you are, if you want to be more uninhibited, I invite you to think about whatever sexual hang-ups you may have, and if you don't like the idea of them seeping into your sex life, I want you to work on getting over those mental hump(s), so you can get back to humping freely again without shame or guilt. Because I can almost guarantee you will keep banging your head on your own sexual glass ceiling (and not in a good way) until you finally deal with your baggage. Until you find a healthy way to transcend your past traumas, you will probably not achieve full "sex god" mode — your bundle of anxieties will make sure of that!

It won't be easy, but if you can just find a way to beat back those ghosts by facing your issues head-on, you will almost surely become a more a present and giving partner, and you'll have better orgasms, too. It all goes back to achieving "wholeness." *Yep, that*

MASTER DATER

again. In the bedroom, it means, not just overcoming past traumas, but being comfortable with your own sexuality and body, because a big part of being "whole" is *you* have to believe you're a sex god.

Ever met someone who wasn't a perfect 10 physically, but was still super sexy? Think, peak Angelica Huston and Jack Nicholson when they were a couple. Jack and Angie were not your typical gorgeous specimens, but they both had tremendous sex appeal, right? Well, you can too. It's all about your attitude and less about how you shake your booty (though that helps). I honestly can't tell you how hot simple body confidence can be. It can be even sexier than beauty, power, money, fame, all of that.

So, get to know your body!

A tingly way to do it is by getting reacquainted with yourself by taking some time to explore your body in the privacy of your home with your hands, fingers, toys, whatever — so you know what you like (and don't). That way, when the time comes, you'll be able to communicate your needs to your partner.

Now, if you're on a mission to transform yourself from a ho-hum lover to a tantric sex dynamo, here are a few more bedroom moves that will give some added juice to your sexual intimacy, no matter how long you and your partner have been getting freaky.

1. Make Time for Medium Petting — When all touch leads to sex, it can be easier for your lover to keep a distance when they're not feeling it. Many women do this, so they aren't giving mixed signals to their horny partners. Try making a place for medium petting like kissing, rubbing, massaging, hand jobs, feel-ups, or whatever else you can come up with that doesn't involve penis to vagina penetration. Because when a woman feels distant from their lover, it makes it harder to segue into those more sweaty desires you're always dreaming about. Sometimes you really can give less, to get more.

2. Yeoman Sex Can Be A Godsend — To keep your sex bond strong, try mixing in some *yeoman* sex. I'm not talking about a threesome with a salty pirate! Yeoman sex is simply survival sex that gets the job done. You may not win any sexual Heisman Trophy's but when a couple has lower expectations for every sexual encounter, it results in better attendance in bed. So don't shoot for porn star sex every time because who needs that kind of performance anxiety? Yeoman sex will also help you avoid the ego bruising, "sex avoidance," which can ruin anyone's love life. And sometimes isn't it nice to feel wanted, please a partner, and have a quickie, without all the hoopla? *Guys, don't answer that.*

3. Unlock Your Mental Chastity Belt — As a Bunny Ranch sex worker once said, "Foreplay starts before you open the bedroom door." It's one of the best pieces of sex advice I've ever heard. Take it to heart and you've just unlocked the key to satisfying your partner (and yourself). If your mind is your biggest sex organ (and it is), unlock your mental chastity belt, and let your imagination get you all hot and bothered. Having sexual fantasies about another man, woman, or even five gnomes tying you to a bedpost doesn't mean you're a cheater, or a sick freak. OK, the gnome thing is a bit odd, but whatever. It's all in your head! That's why they call them fantasies! And by sharing your sex fantasies with your lover, it can keep your erotic vibe alive, and will likely improve your sex game, too.

4. Milk the Afterglow — After sex, do you ever get up, go to the bathroom and simply go about your day — *Ho-hum, another orgasm*–leaving your lover in bed like a cold fish in a bucket? I'm guilty of it, too. We've all probably heard the boilerplate post coitus lines from partners like " ... *I think it's going to rain* ... " or had a post sex letdown when our man turns over and commences snoring loudly while we're still trying to relish all our body sensations. These emotionless moves can turn an intense physical connection into an immediate disconnection, fast. So, work on staying present. And work on your pillow talk, it will help keep the erotica alive, and deepen your intimacy level. Remember, your lover is likely emotionally raw after sex, and offering you a soul glimpsing moment, so take note! Who knows, you may even talk them into an overtime "O" as a reward?

5. Screw An Erection? You Don't Always Need It! –This may hurt some men to hear this but you really don't need an erection to have a good time in bed. I'm not saying boners are useless (oh, we like them). But you can't force a man to have an erection if his body is not cooperating, especially older dudes. So, give it some time to flourish by defining your sex sessions more broadly, and including lots of heavy petting, massage, touch, and sensual talk into your bedroom. If you take your time, erections can come and go and come again (hello vicar!) And with so many body parts to play with, why should we limit ourselves to one joystick?

6. Don't Always Trust a Boner — Ever gotten hard or wet by something that has nothing to do with sex? You're not some weirdo, it's actually a phenomenon called "arousal non-concordance." It's when your body can appear aroused (with a rock hard erection, or super wet vulva) but you're not even turned on. So, to make sure your mate is in the mood for love, a simple verbal confirmation will confirm what your body thinks your partner wants. Just remember to ask because our naughty bits can actually be deceiving.

7. Check Your Mood Math — If you or your partner are just not feeling it, look around and see if you have more distractions going than turn-ons, because that is often the problem. You may be lying next to a hot partner with lots of coconut oil dripping from their nipples, but if you look down and the dog is licking your toes? Or you're stressed out about life, work, or afraid your roommate is going to barge-in any minute? Check your mood math and try again when the time is right. It doesn't take an algebra genius to know that letting the dog in on the licking can kill the sex buzz! Unless you're into that sort of thing, then let Fido lick away.

It seems so much of success in life is simply about showing up and giving it your best shot, while staying open, positive, and ready to play, right? The bedroom is no different. If you're determined to transform from a neurotic ice queen into a white-hot sex animal overnight, experiment with different sex positions, different forms of touch, or foreplay like withholding orgasm, erotic timing, sexual fantasies, and role play. Do it until you find your "go-to sex move" that makes you rise up off the bed, screaming for more. The same goes for your love — you want to please them, too! Just know there's no magic bullet solution. Both women and men have such unique sex drives with individual rhythms and tastes that it's impossible to please everyone with these tips. So, please take them as inspiration, kind of like a sexual Pinterest board, and let it serve as a reminder that sex is an essential part of our lives. Because when you're able to seamlessly blend your eroticism into the fabric of who you are, you will begin to feel more grounded, and safer with your clothes off. And once you have a steady sexual foundation, you may find you're no longer making time to have sex because your sexuality is always there, boiling over, ready to pounce at a moment's notice. Improving your sex life should be an ongoing project. But it honestly doesn't matter how many new positions you know, how waxed or toned you are, or how hot your partner thinks you are — if *you* don't believe it, you're not going to perform like the uninhibited sex machine you want to be. So, throw all that baggage overboard, own your own sexuality, and go have some fun while your body is still a wonderland, and not a bargain basement bin!

23 I Feel Safe with You
Love's Secret Ingredient

We can all probably remember a past relationship when we felt so comfortable with our partners that it made all the difference in the world. When you've got a good egg that you can take home to Mom, who actually makes you hot in the bedroom, too? It can feel like you hit the jackpot. He loves you AND you can tell them anything? *Sign me up.* I know if I feel comfortable making some crazy joke, or exposing some silly personal imperfection to my main squeeze, and he doesn't judge me for being weird? Then I feel safe with him, at least on some level. It may not be as hot as porn star sex, but the power of safety in a relationship is a real thing.

Yet, today I feel like the common sentiment is to dump any partner who seems safe, because they must be boring drips who will suck your life force and saddle you with kids for all eternity, which is not *entirely* true. Safe lovers can be awesome partners, who are quite (ahem) attentive in bed. too! Call me the awkward tomboy who had the hots for the sweet, yet mysterious art kid back in junior high (he was hot, seriously), but I've found if you only date people you feel safe around, you often have pretty good luck. Is that boring to admit? Maybe, but who cares, if it works?? Feeling safe is the difference between having an intimate relationship, and just a fleeting, transactional (usually sexual) one. Safe partners don't have to agree on everything, but you should feel comfortable bringing anything up in a conversation, even those dusty skeletons in your closets! Does this sound like a relationship you want to be in? Sure, it does, or it should. Does anyone ever want to be in a deceptive relationship?

Only if they are the person doing the deceiving.

In safe relationships, we can reveal our vulnerabilities and true selves. Sometimes, it can feel so natural, that we will take a safe lover for granted. But resist that urge. If you are in a trusting safe relationship, you've already discovered one part of being human that makes life so beautiful — *being loved for being yourself.* So, consider yourself fortunate.

It's not just on the "woke" partner's shoulders to make the relationship feel safe. Both partners must play a role in constantly checking in on the relationship's emotional safety level. While one partner may feel vulnerable one day; the other person may not realize their own manic energy is making matters worse. So, this couple better be able to communicate their feelings freely, or the resentments will start to pile up. It can get even messier when one person's vulnerability triggers another person's vulnerability — then you've got a drama queen festival. Claws out! If this happens and defenses are raised, it can lead to brutal verbal slugfests, which spoils the safe feeling this couple had been building.

One massive barrier to establishing a safe relationship environment today, is a ton of people have decided, even when they fall in love, to keep their public persona walls up far longer than I feel is healthy. So, if you're looking to make an intimate vulnerable connection on a blind date, I'd stay home and watch *The Notebook* instead, because you're probably not getting it on OK Cupid! This is not a scientific survey, but I bet you could have 10 online dates today, and never really get to know any of them, because *we never take off our public personas anymore — we live in them.*

Which is terrifying for the future of intimacy in America. "Hey, I met this dude on Tinder, who is he really? NO idea! So, I guess I better keep my guard up forever, and pretend I have it all together, just in case he's the one." How backwards is that logic? Most people go into a relationship *wanting* to be honest, transparent, and secure. But due to our histories, fragile egos, and (yes) hot tempers — putting on masks, and putting up walls (even in the bedroom) is the new way to make us feel safe with this strange rando that we just met online.

Even if the idea of revealing your vulnerabilities to the world makes you cringe, you don't have to hide your soft spots forever. You can change, and you kind of have to, if you want to find THE ONE. If you can put in the effort to establish an intimacy level early on in a relationship, all of these walls can come tumbling down. Once a couple can get real with each other and say, *"We both bring emotional garbage and old scars to this coupling. We both have hurt each other's feelings without knowing it. But if we can have an emotional safe place in the relationship, it will help us to fix our hurtful miscommunications,"* they will have a much higher chance of surviving.

Now, if the emotional safety is just not there, it's almost impossible to get over a fight, so the hurt and resentments keep piling up for day, weeks, months, even years. You can bet this lingering resentment (if not resolved) will come up again in the next fight, or by passive-aggressive stonewalling, criticism, or just flat out leaving the relationship. A secure relationship will forgive us for all the garbage we bring to the table. Once you have gotten through some conflict in a healthy way, it can make your coupling feel closer and more secure. You'll say to yourself, "Wow, they didn't even bring up any old fights or issues." Why? Because they've healed from them and moved on! That's what good eggs do.

Emotional safety always goes both ways. It's how secure you are (and how you see the world) as well as what kind of environment you provide your lover. Is it a safe space, or is it a place where you may judge or hurt them? The goal is to provide a safe place for both partners. And if you want your partner to bare their soul, lean into your vulnerabilities, and drop your public mask, too! Dare to be yourself in all your flawed glory. Hopefully, your partner has provided you with a safe environment where it's easy to be you, because you know you'll be accepted, no matter what you say.

Now, you may be wondering, "How can I provide an emotionally safe environment for my partner?" It's a great question! First, as stated, you need to look at your own flaws. Are you creating a safe environment that allows people to feel like they can tell you anything? We are often unaware that our (unapproachable, or un-receptive) aura is what invites people to withhold information or put up a mask around us. Without knowing how we affect people, we may accidentally magnify someone else's insecurities, which creates more distance!

Of course, it takes two to tango. We can't control others; but we can control ourselves. So, I encourage you to set the stage for an emotional safe space with your bae. Be mindful of your judgements and criticisms. Kindly inquire if they pull away from you, and reassure your lover with words like, *"I hope you know you can tell me about your family. I think you are amazing, and whatever happened in your past has given you great character."*

In a perfect world, we would all be less judgmental and open to addressing our insecurities, but just because we're not that evolved yet, doesn't mean we can't keep trying because creating a non-judgmental environment for your lovers can be life-altering. So, even if you're not close to revealing your flaws to anyone, you have to keep working on being whole, and leaning on your support network of friends, so you feel confident enough in your own skin to keep your walls down, as much as possible.

The reasons for unsafe air between couples can be so complex. Whatever unspoken issues you have is probably standing in the way of you getting any closer. Your baggage is like this sumo-sized skeleton in bed with you; it makes it really hard to love someone the way you want, if you've got that fat bastard in between you 24/7. So, on that note, here are some more tips for conjuring that "safe and easy" feeling in your relationship!

1. Validate When They Open Up — No quick judgements. Show compassion.

2. Practice Open Body Language — Maintain eye contact. NO multitasking.

3. Be a Reflective Listener — Don't punish them with emotional outbursts, LISTEN

4. Keep the Environment Safe — Be honest and open so they continue being honest

Figure Out What's Going On — Try asking questions like, "Are there things you wish you could tell me but are afraid to?" If they say "Yes,' Ask them, "What would it feel like to share that with me?"

Fostering emotional safety plays out (not just on first dates) but throughout the lifetime of a relationship. Forget sex, money and common hobbies, safety is the secret to happiness in any stage of a relationship! When a couple feels safe, they have the potential to deepen their connection until they have an unbreakable emotional bond. But when someone feels like they will be judged (or misunderstood) it can create all sorts of roadblocks for happiness.

So, pay attention to how you, and your lover feel and share, before you get more entangled with things like marriage and 2.5 kids. And never be afraid to share your biggest dreams and fears with each other because a couple that is vulnerable and compassionate together, usually stays together!

24 The Language and Shorthand of Lasting Love

Become Fluent in Your Partner's Unique Emotional Lingo

Wouldn't it be amazing if every person you met came with a warning label? *Warning: One serving of Sally, contains riotous laughter, daddy issues, a light stalking tendency, and is defensive when confronted with her faults?* Sounds like a Charlie Kaufman movie, right? But if human warning labels were a real thing, I imagine we would all probably feel safer dating strangers, and would start choosing our partners based on our actual needs, rather than by some hot sexy thing's tight outer package, which (as we all know) are often ridiculously deceiving.

As tough and independent as we all like to think we are, deep down under our polished outer personas, we all have emotional needs. Just like our bodies need sunlight, food and water, every human heart requires love and compassion to stick around this planet for the long-term. Without love, we literally "check out" much sooner than people who are in long relationships. Knowing all this, isn't it peculiar how so many people are still too afraid to ask for the love they need?? After all, our vulnerable request might get rejected, which makes it that much more precarious. So, many people today will bury what they think are their embarrassing and squishy emotional needs (or save them for their therapists). Something as simple as, "I really need a hug right now," can get passed over until the person meet someone special that gives them a solid emotional safety net, where they feel they can say anything (see Chapter 23).

But even in these safe relationships, words can be misinterpreted. Body language can be confused. Sometimes you may ask for what you need, and still not receive it. What happened? He was such a good listener! When we're happy and in love, we all fantasize that our partners must be reading our minds, or we wouldn't love them in the first place. Um, that sounds great, but it's probably not true! Perhaps this mass delusion (a lot of lovers fall for) is a romantic dream we all share because we all want to hook up with our emotional clones?? I don't know, but until we meet our emotional clones who can read our minds (which, let's face it, will never happen) we have to take matters into our own hands, and change this fantasy narrative ourselves.

Even the healthiest couples have to constantly work on their communication.

You can't play games, or give off subtle clues and expect to have your mind-read by your lover — because psychic lovers don't exist. Unless you're married to Miss Cleo or David Blaine you don't have that luxury, so don't expect it. Once you realize you have to make your voice heard (to get what you want emotionally), you will probably start to get more of what you need — I said probably. *You may have to say it a few times.*

The good news is lots of couples are able to develop an emotional shorthand (or lingo) to keep their intimacy and love burning white-hot. They may use inside jokes, or pet names for each other to constantly reaffirm their love. Or say, "I love you" every time they say goodbye. Or habitually ask about each other's dreams and passions, and then shut up and listen! That is what I call "next level emotional listening," which can take years to develop, so don't assume it will happen overnight. You really have to work on it, but once you have it down, it can be the best and stickiest relationship glue around.

I know a couple who has worked on it for years, and now, they both give fantastic lover's shorthand. Every time they have a conflict, they'll start every conversation with, *"I need you to listen to me fully before you start talking. I want to hear you, but I want you to hear me out first."* Other times, the woman in the couple will say, *"I need you to support me right now. I don't want advice. I just need you let me vent."* Every woman feels this way, guys!

Besides conflict resolution, having a strong relationship lingo allows you to lovingly (and non-violently, a big key) express your needs to your partner in a way that is inclusive and compassionate to both perspectives. It won't always be smooth sailing, but if you can learn how to weave inclusion and compassion into your love shorthand, you'll be setting yourself up for a long run that could become marriage (one day) if that's important to you.

Setting up your own unique lingo that you both understand will take some self-knowledge and practice. If you're not all that comfortable voicing your needs, it may feel awkward at first, but if you are both open and patient, you'll eventually get the hang of it. Once you do, you'll see it really is a magical relationship skill that can guide you and your squeeze to be the loving and safe partners that always knew you could be. And who doesn't want that??

25 Wearing Black Forever Is Never A Good Look

Moved on From a Blah Relationship? Great, Now Get Back Out There!

There is no right way to grieve a breakup. There is no ideal timetable, and no perfect blueprint approved by Oprah, but a little soul-searching can go a long way. Reflecting on a lost love affair can help us to reset our emotional compass, objectively process what went wrong, solidify lessons learned, and get back to being ourselves. So, a little mourning is a good thing, but you can't wear black forever. Perpetual cave-dwelling can be harmful to your health; seriously, leave the hibernating to the bears, and I don't mean the hairy gay men! As much as your heartbreak hurts, I will wager that you broke up with him (or her) for a very good reason. Perhaps you finally stood up, and said, "I'm not settling for this blah relationship, I want more!" Bravo.

Now the hard part is over; *say hello to the rest of your life.*

But moving on is never that simple for women, why? One reason is we tend to blame ourselves for failed relationships, even when the breakup is 100% the other person's fault. Before you get back into the dating scene, it may be valuable to spend some time ridding yourself of your self-blaming tendencies, especially if you're the type who always says it was just "bad timing," or you were not "good enough, or loveable enough, or not pretty, smart, or funny enough," rather than telling the unvarnished truth, like they cheated, lied, or falsely projected crap on you that wasn't true! You may think you're keeping your personal life private by "playing nice" and blaming yourself, but all that covering up is just a defense mechanism to avoid the painful reality of what actually happened.

If you realize you have self-blaming tendencies, I encourage you to examine how you frame breakups (to yourself and the world), because how you explain your breakups will affect your future love life. Instead of beating yourself up, see if you can adopt a *growth mindset*; in dating terms, it means that you acknowledge, "Yes, I've made mistakes but I will learn from them; I'm not broken or worthless, I'm just a human growing from life, and I deserve love."

If you can get to that mental space, and really believe it?

Guess, what? You are probably ready to date again because we all need people in our lives, *whether we like them or not!* This doesn't mean we *must date* to fill some internal void; but we kinda do … at some point, like maybe, right now? No pressure, go ahead, and put your own time table on your return. But, please, don't wait until you grow hair in strange places and your naughty bits shrivel up … After all, your soul mate is waiting.

I have known a lot of skeptical (recently divorced) people who had to be dragged out of the house to go on a new date, but they were so happy they did! You may not realize it, but we humans often heal our emotional wounds by being around other people. It doesn't come by taking handfuls of mood-altering pills, banging strangers online, or isolating ourselves in caves of regret! We're like these well-groomed pack animals who need to be around our packs to feel alive. So, are you ready to give your pack of humanity another shot?

If you feel like dating again, but you're concerned you'll talk about your ex the whole time, or will be thinking about them constantly — perhaps *it's not the right time to get out there?* If you find yourself in a room full of gorgeous, interesting people, but to you, they all look like they're infested with a deadly strain of Ebola — *perhaps it's still time to wait?*

If you're stuck in a grieving cycle, think about the longing you feel. Are you confusing missing your ex with missing *someone?* Remember, our memories are not always reliable sources. Our brains have a sneaky way of making our past lovers seem way better than they actually were. So, tread gently on your nostalgia, and figure out if those lingering feelings are for your ex, or for the warm body and nice companion that you miss? Warm companions to share your bed with are great, but you can get that from a dog! So, don't mourn an old ex that a new pet can easily replace. (Okay, that is a bit harsh . But you know what I mean.) You will also know when you've moved past your mourning stage when you don't miss them anymore. *You'll just want to see them dead! (J/K)*

Now, if you ever find yourself at some party and you're feeling attracted to everyone around you, and you can't even remember your ex's name? Hello Dolly, it may be time to add some new dates to your social calendar! I said *several.* Remember, your dream partner (Ryan or Oliva) never shows up on your first date. So, if you're looking for dream-boat quality, you will have to cast a wider net. And unless you unfortunately clicked on the next Ted Bundy's Bumble profile, you will most likely survive a single date!

So, take a deep breath, get yourself together and (at least) get your toes wet. After you've survived your first date (which you probably made a huge deal of in your head) you will know if you're ready to date, or not. If you still feel anxious about dating (uh, join the club). Just see if you can differentiate between your *dating anxiety* and your actual *readiness to date again*. If you really listen to yourself, you'll know if you're into dating again, or it's just a distraction to ease your pain. Even if you decide you're not ready, nudging yourself out to date would probably be a good for you at some point!

I invite you to gently push yourself a little to get you out of your solo routine. It's totally natural for people we love to stay in our hearts, especially if they dumped us while we still loved them. That's fine; let them stay there. BUT when you go back into the world, you have to forget about them, so you can date, flirt and, yes, have sex without bringing your ex with you, because who wants to date you, and your ex's ghost? Maybe a few kinky Ghostbusters, but THAT'S IT.

26 Like in Life and Souffles — Timing Is Everything

Rebounds, Pull Backs and Other Dating Maneuvers (If That's Your Thing)

As awesome as true love can be, humans don't actually *need* life partners to feel fulfilled. Sure, they are great to have around, but I know quite a few people who have flown solo their entire lives, and seem to be perfectly happy being alone. So, I don't want to order anyone to go fall in love right now, dammit! Because there are many good reasons that a new love affair would not be important to you. Your life may be too jam packed with friends and activities. Or you may be dealing with a health issue, or have young children, and feel it's not the right time to explore a new love, or you may have a stressful job (or a hobby) that takes up all your time. Depending on your situation, those may be excuses, or real legitimate reasons for not dating — only you know!

If you've mined your soul for clarity, and you still aren't sure if you're ready to dive back into the bone zone, you can always try dating again, and then pull back if it's totally unpleasant — nothing is permanent! Regardless of whether you go for it now, or not, I really hope you can conjure some positive feelings about relationships. I'm not assuming you're some Debbie Downer but all men and women do not suck! We all don't have virulent smallpox!

But that said, the timing for your return to dating is entirely up to you. You can wait until you find the right person, or you can swing from one relationship to the next — I don't judge. I just want you to be happy. We are social creatures who need emotional support in our lives, which is interesting, because have you noticed? Our day-to-day environments often lack any sort of community to rely on? Sooooo, we have to find people we can trust in this world, which often leads to intimate loving relationships because those often provide the deepest connections.

Being a psychotherapist, I always think, "Wouldn't it be great if every broken-hearted person could take all the time they needed to grieve, and really feel what it's like to be alone BEFORE they courted another lover? That sounds great, but come on — life is never that clean! As we get older and hopefully wiser, I feel like most of us realize that life can get messy and that's okay — bring on the mess if it's going to make us smile!

If you are still stuck a deep, dark love rut, I encourage you to quit bashing yourself about what you "should have" done. The past is over, babe. Healing that pain you've been carrying around can happen through therapy, meditation, exercise, or through other people — or NOT. Hiding out in a cave of solitude may heal one person while it makes another person stir crazy! So, be gentle on yourself and know that we all have different emotional needs. As Dolly Parton sang so eloquently, *"The best way to get over a lover is to get under another."* I cannot unequivocally validate (or disprove) Dolly's quote here but I'm not going to be critical of it, either! Everyone gets a kick out of different things. Sometimes rebounds are hot mess disasters, while other times, they can turn out to be healing relationships that are not rebounds at all. They become life partners! So quiet that internal critic who thinks they know best, and perhaps, allow yourself to be surprised by someone, because, sometimes life has a mysterious way of working out — if we are open to it.

27 Doomed to Dating Douchebags?

Dating Is Not A Horror Show Unless You Make It One

In a planet full of 7.4 billion beating hearts, it's kind of heart-breaking that we can't all find true love. Sadly, most of us don't even come close! I've heard plenty of people utter this shocking revelation in my life, *"I have never had a healthy relationship."* Or another version of the same tune: *"I have never had a real relationship."* Really? *Never?* Whenever I meet one of these people, I gently inquire about the possibility of them "getting back out there." Do you want to hear the popular refrain I get a lot to-day? *"What's the point? I'm sure I'm just going to end up dating more douchebags again."*

Has it gotten this bad, ladies of the free world?

Is there really a d-bag lurking around every corner?

Whenever I ask my single friends, they often reply, "Um, yeaaah, d-bags are everywhere." So, if that's really true, how should one tender-hearted soul even begin looking for love in a world seemingly bereft of suitable partners? This topic might take an entire book to explain! But I feel like the underlying issue here is pretty common. The world is actually not overrun by douchebags, but it certainly feels that way for a lot of people, women especially,

an opportunity to show off how great a partner you can be!

So, spray a light mist of douche repellant on (before your next date if you must) and give your heart a second chance to connect with someone worthy of your love. Because there are always new people to date, no matter where you live. That's what great about being human. Millions of beating hearts are out there right now just waiting to give you some healthy loving; I'm serious! Can you hear them? Quiet your mind: *Ba-bump-ba-bump*. See? They're out there just waiting to find another heart that beats in perfect harmony with theirs, so what are you waiting for? Follow the sounds of those beating hearts!

28 Never Give Up on Cupid, No Matter How Late the Bastard Is

Going Back to the Wishing
Well One More Time

Ever known someone who was hurt badly in a relationship, and never seemed to bounce back? There could be many reasons for this (some extremely traumatic) so I want to gently exclude abuse survivors from this conversation since I could sadly write an entire book, just for them (and I may one day). But for now, let's talk about people who brand themselves as "victims," after having a few sure, kind of bad, yet (in the grand scheme) fairly benign failed relationships. We've all probably met one of these people. Is it too harsh to call them Trauma Queens? Because the longer they allow themselves to live with that emotional distress (like it happened yesterday), the more it becomes part of their primary life narrative. *"The S.O.B. left me. Look at me now; they took the best years of my life; I will never love again!"* Oh dear.

To these poor pitiful Petunias, that one relationship became a permanent roadblock to any future happiness. What happened to their hope? What happened to their libidos? We will never know what's truly happening inside every persons' heart — so it's impossible to know. But I feel like there are steps we can take to get over a breakup that is much healthier than holding on to a grudge, forever. Did you know people who rebound from break-ups the best often mourn the dead relationship before it's even over? It's true, these "early mourners" often find themselves dating again earlier than they thought (mainly) because they already mourned their last breakup *while they were ending the relationship!*

Pretty smart, isn't it? I thought so …

As for people who jump right back into the dating game after a breakup, just because you're having sex with an entire volleyball team on Tinder doesn't mean you're "over" your ex, guys! Lots of people use dating as a distraction to ease the pain of their last breakup, which (sure) may fill their empty bed with lots of warm volleyball playing bodies, but their emotional emptiness echoes inside, until they deal with that ringing void inside.

Besides the "early rebound daters," there are other people who get so stunned by a surprise breakup, that they wallow in denial, and order up an IV drip of Wellbutrin and Gin and Tonics (not a combo I'd recommend) for as long as the can get away with it, doing anything they can to avoid being honest with themselves about their own sadness (and culpability in the breakup). Perhaps, they were left mentally scrambling to put the pieces together. Whatever reason, I've noticed a ton of people will just stuff old relationships away, never mourning them at all, until years later, when some skeleton rears its ugly head to remind them, like a zombie from a horror movie. "Not them again. I thought I was done with them?!" To quote the love-struck movie Magnolia, *"You may be through with the past but the past isn't through with you."*

If you're now thinking you MAY have mourned a past lover a wee bit too long, I gently encourage you to take a step back, and see if you can internalize some lessons from your breakup.

Whatever was the cause, it really doesn't matter now. The relationship is over, so you can't let yourself walk around with "bleeding emotional wounds," and bleed all over any new person you might be romantically interested in, and expect them to lap it up, unless you're into dating ER nurses, or Red Cross volunteers! No one wants to hear about emotional wounds on a first date. NO ONE. So, a wounded person must take time to heal, and absorb what they've learned, before getting back out there. *But you DO have to get back out there. You can't give up on cupid no matter how late that little bastard is!*

Because I believe that you (yes, you!) deserve to have a new healthy and passionate new love in your life. Who cares if you've been "unlucky in love," so far? Don't let some past ex ruin your present and your future; they already screwed up your past, right? So, let's draw the line right here, because that hot freaking ghost has haunted you long enough!

If it makes you feel better, I, too, have been haunted by a hot ghost. Mine had a flowing man bun, so it's that much more embarrassing! It began as a childhood crush then became a full-on love affair that really affected me. Probably because he was one of those dreamy Italian "futbal" players that tells you how beautiful you are over red wine at some café. Sigh. Swoon, gush. I was head over high heels for the man bun! My handsome prince was a rare combo of kind, gentle, artistic, and fun to be around. Our youth and my naivety (we had no idea what we were doing) led to us lovingly part ways after some time. I was an emotional mess for a while, but when I got back to dating again, it took me a while before I realized, "Oh no, I'm dating anyone that resembles my long-lost man bun!" If some random guy had long black hair with an artistic flair? Sure, let's go out! What? You're into soccer and making ceramic pottery?

Well, meow to you too, signore, do tell!

Obviously, I was not over him.

I was grasping for fragments of my long-lost dreamboat in other people, and when I found something that reminded me of "him," (physically or mentally) you can bet, I sucked whatever that thing was dry like the last freaking bone marrow on earth (pun fully intended!). I was holding on to my sexy ghost for dear life. I was so hopelessly hooked on the memory of my Italian man bun that I couldn't see I was projecting him on all my current lovers like Jimmy Stewart in the movie Vertigo. OK, maybe not that obsessive. But it was close!

You may think "chasing ghost lovers" is the stuff of movies, but it's pretty common in dating. That's why so many people have a "specific type" they're attracted to (like my affinity for Italian soccer players). Enchanting first loves can linger in our minds for forever, playing games with our heads, and teasing us into magnifying the positives of some Bro-Hunk with a man bun that we met in our dodgeball league who (sure) could pass for our lost love's stunt double, but he's not him! He plays freaking dodgeball, and look at his man bun, it's a mess!

Sigh. Can you see what I'm saying here?

Unless you're into dating people who look like ghosts from your past, why not leave these "replicant relationships" behind, and see if you can find a whole new type of sexy to get your engine purring? Forget about all those late-night regrets that have haunted your past, and find a new tune to sing! Resist the urge to stir up any remaining, *"What if we got back together? Would it work this time if I changed?"* scenarios that can reverberate in our minds, because there is no going back to yesterday!

I know, here's a hankie. It can be heart wrenchingly painful. I empathize. It can take some time to make sense of it all. So, give yourself time, and grieve a breakup properly, don't run from the pain. My hope is every healing heart reading this learns how to play a more positive narrative in their minds about all your past relationships, so you can get back to dating again with no lingering ghosts with man buns hanging around!

Um, am I talking to myself here?... I'll never tell (until the next chapter).

Every breakup is different. There is no timer that goes off in our heads that says, "Ding! I'm ready to bang again!" Although, that would be an awesome timer, especially for guys. We all strive to "get our shit" together, which is not a psychotherapist's clinical term, but we all know what that means! So, let's be totally honest: we're all a little neurotic underneath (which is a generous understatement for many people). So, it's OK to be a little fractured and flawed, that is what makes us human. And for some heartbroken people, they will never be *"ready"* to date again, and for them, that is OK.

BUT my guess is you picked up this book because you're not ready to retire from the dating scene, just yet. You're ready, perhaps more than you think, to try dating again. That is a great sign! If you feel guilty for throwing a good lover away, own that feeling, and then let it go. Sure, you may have totally screwed up a great relationship (it happens to all of us), but you can learn from your mistakes right now, and grow from them, so you don't end up repeating them with a new lover. And that's what it takes to truly get over any heartbreak: *emotional growth*.

29 Dreams Can Come True, If You Squint Your Eyes a Little

Out of your Comfort Zone is Where All the Magic Truly Happens

Admit it: are your buns tingly after sitting on the edge-of-your-seat since Chapter freakin' 2, wondering what the blazes happened to that mysterious blind date situation? *Welllll* ... he didn't end up being a sleazy car salesman, or a colossal douchebag, after all. Can you believe a decade later, he remains one of the most ethical and funniest people I've ever met? You can't say that about many blind dates. You also can't (often) say that the guy, which I had to be semi-shamed into blind dating, *is now my husband.* What a plot twist if I do say so my ... *what??* You saw that twist coming the whole time? Bah! I'm no good at surprises!!

But this revelation certainly surprised me.

I wasn't expecting to find "my man" on any blind date, but it seems fairly common these days. A staggering number of couples today of all ages are getting happily entwined, hitched (or what have you) after meeting on blind dates, which hello, are what dating apps are! If you want proof, just glance at the wedding announcements in *The New York Times.* An entire generation is hooking up blindly. So, I guess I don't feel so strange about it anymore. Looking back, my blind dating success only happened after I finally got "whole" again (Chapter 8). I really took the time I needed to get over my man bun lover (Chapter 28) which took a lot of painful introspection. I also worked on my own flawed self! I realized I had to deal with all my past issues, traumas, and skeletons, that were holding me down. It wasn't easy, those ghosts and skeletons have tight, bony grips! But I did it, which I suppose, is what you call evolving into the person I wanted to be, to attract the type of person I wanted to attract? Yeah, that sounds about right.

Plus. I also got lucky. I just did.

That blind date could have easily been with another soulless banker or trust fund d-bag, but fortune smiled on me that day. My future hubs was confident (maybe crazy) enough to appreciate all my quirks that makes me so darn "special" (which others may call so "disturbed") like my sardonic Carrie Fisher-like sense of humor, my penchant for wearing funky clothes in inappropriate venues, and my off-the-wall creative ideas and strange comments. Oh yeah, and I'm dyslexic. *So, too, that was there* ... That was a dyslexic joke, *WTB*.

By not judging me, he pulled me closer. I resisted, but not for long.

Now, we both feel lucky to be in a passionate, loving, and emotionally safe relationship that keeps getting closer each day. Perhaps meeting later in life (we were both in our 30s), gave us relativity? I don't know, but we already kind of knew how to deal with the many, many imperfections that life gives us, while also being able to fight back our own demons of projection and (false) expectations. Or again, maybe we just got lucky?! We definitely blew past the honeymoon phase years ago, but we still enjoy our deep intimate connection, companionship, and respect that we give each other daily. It's nourishing and life-affirming, and we even have 2 wonderful kids to show for it. Our love is not always peachy, like all marriages, we have our hiccups too. But, to us, being married is fun and easy.

I wish the same for you, one day.

Now that I've humbly shared some concepts that I learned in my dating life, and as being a psychotherapist, I'd like to think you will take some of these choice nuggets with you on your next dating adventure. I'd also like to think you've gained some new perspectives on dating that will lead to even more growth in the future. On that topic, Ralph Waldo Emerson wrote, *"The mind, once stretched by a new idea, never returns to its original dimensions."* My dream for you is your mind has been forever stretched by these new ideas, and that you will take these lessons to heart, and march forward with new insight and a deeper awareness for yourself and the dating world, forever affected by our brief encounter, but in a good way!

Because as much fun as dating can be, it can also be humbling, embarrassing, and take loads of courage to keep at it. But we humans are so very adaptable. We love to learn new tricks. So, I'm wagering it will be really hard for you to read this book, and NOT be a little transformed by what you learned. My grand theory is your next long-term relationship or (even) your next single-serving bang sesh with a sex taxi operator will almost certainly be improved because *you have improved*, and become a better dater, and (yes) potential life partner.

Are you still dubious? You just have to live the question and, trust me!

But that said, don't think for a moment I'm some love guru. You definitely do not want to copy my dating style which was like Annie Hall, meets a bipolar field mouse, meets Linda Blair from The

Exorcist (but again, in a good way!) Thankfully for both of us, we psychotherapists can't make dating decisions for our clients!

In the end, it is going to be up to you to bring this love train home because your life will continue to have its own unique twists, turns, and surprise endings. I wish I could give every beating heart a fail-safe blueprint for success in the love game, but I can't, since there isn't one. But I do hope I've given you some ideas to chew on and, yes, maybe a few to giggle about, too.

Whatever happens on our individual quests for love, while we are being gentle on others, we must remember to be gentle on ourselves, too. Self-compassion is so very necessary, it's the best form of self-medication there is, especially in matters of love. Before we settle down and get married, we often date a string of people. So, when those relationships end, sometimes all we have to sustain ourselves is our own self-love while we stay on the hunt for "the one." So, it's important that we be gentle on ourselves because (hopefully) we are our own biggest fans.

Go ahead, think of something you've done recently that you kind of regret, and forgive yourself for it, right now. Feels great, doesn't it? Because "shit happens" to us all! And it will happen again. Sooooo, unless you just shot an elephant or helped start World War III, just laugh it off, and forgive yourself. *Then give yourself a second chance.* And a third. And a fourth. Ad infinitum! Your support tribe can help you stay on course, but you control the mic of your internal self-critic! So, pull that heckler's plug when he gets too loud, and just be patient with yourself, my sexy little pretties. Love will come knocking. I just know it will.

It takes time and effort to mature into a whole human being. Relativity doesn't fall out of the sky. It must be earned. So, self-compassion is essential because you're not the only one who finds the game of love mysterious, and perplexing! The next "Mr. or

Miss Right Now" you date, may not turn out to be "the one," but who cares? You have a new life experience, and you've hopefully gained new insights along the way, which can only help your prospects of finding your soul mate down the road. So, keep getting out there with your new bad whole self!

Even though I've never met you, I believe you are beautiful and deserving of all the love in the world. In whatever shape, size, or color you come in, there is so much to love in you: inside and out. I know you have a lot of love to give to some lucky soul, so I truly believe you will navigate your love quest a lot better than I did, with probably much less projectile vomiting!

Never forget: you have a bottomless well of love inside of you.

And the more love we have, the more love we have to give. I want to thank you for your open mind, and for spending this time with me. I truly hope our paths will cross in the real world, one day. Until then, may peace and love be with you.

With gratitude,
Tasha

Acknowledgments

I owe a huge thank you to all the people who helped ink this out.

To my family, who let me slack on my domestic duties. Sorry and thank you! A monstrous shout out to Ali M. and self-appointed "#1 fan." Thanks for believing in me, even when I don't, and encouraging me to infuse my humor on the page.

To all my friends and colleagues, who are always game to dive deep into my wacky ideas, provided me marketing insight and stop me from repetitively banging my head on the wall. Particularly, I owe a huge debt of gratitude to Michelle, Kelsey, Adrianne, Mike, Erin, Kory, Racheal, Traci, and Eric.

Murphy Hooker, you have honed your craft to perfection and possess a saintly patience. I was a pain sometimes, but *Master Dater* would be total rubbish without you. Bottom line, I'm honored to have our names together on the cover, and more than that, our friendship that as evolved as a result.

Lastly, to anyone who takes the time to read this, I am touched. Hopefully, you got a few giggles out of it, something to chew on, or in the very least a doorstop. For those that go the extra mile by giving *Master Dater* smashing reviews, telling every person they have ever met, and go buy cargo ship full — well, I am forever indebted. Seriously, thanks for your open mind and heart.

May peace and laughter be with you.

With a diverse clientele that ranges from drag queens to CEOs, San Francisco-based psychotherapist, marriage family therapist and relationships counsellor Tasha Jackson (Fitzgerald) has been widely published in academic journals and has guest lectured as a master-level teacher. Raised by a lesbian mother, Tasha gained national attention for being an early advocate for the LGBTQ community, and was one of the first US-based therapists to openly advocate for gay parenting. Tasha has a master's degree in counselling psychology.

You can connect with her on:
Twitter @TashaJacksTweet
Instagram @Shrink_shots
tashajackson.com

Made in the USA
San Bernardino, CA
02 November 2019